# *Praise for*
# LISTEN YOUR CONSCIENCE

"Living with honor isn't a catchphrase. It's a way of life. *Listen to Your Conscience* provides an insightful and pragmatic path to help you lead a rich and rewarding life. Bravo!"

**NADINE HACK, CEO, beCause Global Consulting**
**Former Board Chair, Desmond Tutu Peace Foundation**

"Want to lead a more meaningful, ethical, and enjoyable life? I strongly recommend that you discover the actionable insights in *Listen to Your Conscience* by revered Frank Sonnenberg."

**KARE ANDERSON**
**Emmy-winning former NBC and *Wall Street Journal* reporter**

"In this delightfully simple and straightforward book, Frank Sonnenberg succeeds in both challenging and compelling us to use our personal power to make the world a happier, healthier place to live, love, work, and play – one conscience choice at a time."

**JOHN E. MICHEL**
**Brig. General USAF (Ret), TED Speaker, C-Suite Leader**

"Frank's book, *Listen to Your Conscience*, encourages you to look deep inside yourself to develop the self-awareness needed to become a better human being. In the process, you'll also find a life filled with joy and contentment."

**LARAE QUY, Former FBI counterintelligence agent**
**Author of *Mental Toughness for Women Leaders* and *Secrets of a Strong Mind***

"Frank Sonnenberg is so much more than an excellent wordsmith. He's a profound thinker who always brings insightful perspective to life's most important issues. *Listen to Your Conscience* is another welcome dose of nutrient-rich food for the soul."

**DR. RODGER DEAN DUNCAN**
**Bestselling author of *CHANGE-friendly LEADERSHIP***

*Praise for*

# LISTEN TO YOUR CONSCIENCE

"Absolutely fantastic! There is so much wisdom in *Listen to Your Conscience* that I promise you will cherish this book as one of the best you have ever read."

**JOHN SPENCE**
**"Among Top 500 Leadership Development Experts in the World" — HR.com**

"*Listen to Your Conscience* is a treasure trove of insights that will help you shape your outlook on living your life with greater purpose and honesty."

**JOHN BALDONI**
**Globally recognized thought leader, Marshall Goldsmith 100 Coach, and author of more than a dozen books.**

"Frank Sonnenberg's new book, *Listen to Your Conscience*, helps today's leaders find a place of centeredness and inner peace in a time of trouble and uncertainty. A breath of fresh air!"

**STEVE GUTZLER**
**President of Leadership Quest**

"Frank has a unique ability to touch the deepest, truest, hidden parts of our minds and hearts in order to inspire change. There's nothing truer or deeper than connecting to your conscience."

**SARAH HINER**
**President and CEO, Bottom Line Inc.**

"In *Listen to Your Conscience*, Frank Sonnenberg has once again brought us back to the basics. Frank is not just teaching us how to craft our life stories, but how to earn credibility, respect, and trust."

**MARK S. BABBITT**
**CEO and Founder, YouTern**

# LISTEN TO YOUR CONSCIENCE

*That's Why You Have One*

FRANK SONNENBERG

Copyright © 2020 by Frank Sonnenberg. All rights reserved. Except as permitted by law, no part of this publication may be reproduced, stored in a database or retrieval system or distributed in any form, in whole or in part, by any means, electronic, mechanical, photocopying, recording, or otherwise, without the prior written permission of the copyright holder. To request permission, please email frank@franksonnenbergonline.com.

Printed in the United States of America.

ISBN: 9798654191465

Kindle Direct Publishing, Seattle, Washington, United States

Cover and interior design by Carrie Ralston, Simple Girl Design LLC.

TO MY WIFE, AND BEST FRIEND, CARON
*Marrying you is the best decision I ever made.
I'm still in love with you after 40 years.*


TO CATHERINE, ERIC, KRISTINE, AND JOHN
*At the end of the day, if you're not proud of who you are and
the way you choose to live your life, little else matters.*


TO CHARLIE, ADDISON, AND JAMES
*Anything is possible when you believe.*

# CONTENTS

**ACKNOWLEDGMENTS**     IX

**INTRODUCTION: ARE YOU BLURRING THE DISTINCTION BETWEEN RIGHT AND WRONG?**     XIX

**LIFE LESSONS**     1

| | |
|---|---|
| Inner Peace Is a Choice | 3 |
| Take Ownership by Taking Responsibility | 7 |
| Never Lower Your Personal Standards. Never! | 11 |
| Is Your Glass Half-Full or Half-Empty? | 15 |
| Are You Inflexible and Stuck in Your Ways? | 19 |
| Do You Deserve to Be Trusted? | 23 |
| 15 Common Myths About Building Trust | 27 |
| Would You Do Something Unethical If You Could Get Away with It? | 31 |
| Ever Feel Like You've Been Taken? | 35 |
| How Credible Are You? | 39 |
| What Does It Take to Be Kind? | 43 |
| Are You Helping People Become Helpless? | 47 |
| Don't Quit. Show Some Grit | 51 |
| How Well Do You Really Know Yourself? | 55 |
| How Do You React to Negative Feedback? | 59 |
| 30 Habits That Create Enormous Distress | 63 |
| The Costs of a Big Ego | 67 |
| Is Your Confidence Turning into Egotism? | 71 |
| Are You a Hypocrite? | 75 |
| When You're a Perfectionist, Your Work Is Never Done | 79 |
| You Deserve It, But… | 83 |
| Do You Let Envy Get the Better of You? | 87 |
| Are You Running Out of Patience? | 91 |
| How to Make Your Words Meaningful | 95 |

| | |
|---|---|
| Here's an Important Message for You | 99 |
| Are You Grateful? | 103 |
| Do You Live in the Dark? | 107 |
| Are You Sabotaging Your Success? | 111 |
| Step Up Your Game | 115 |
| You Can't Force People to Change | 119 |
| Protect Yourself from Bad Information | 123 |
| How to Add More Hours to Your Day | 127 |
| Distractions, Disruptions, and Other Time-Wasters | 131 |
| Good Times Don't Last Forever | 135 |
| How Well Do You Handle Life's Ups and Downs? | 139 |
| Read This Before It's Too Late | 143 |
| Is Your Friend Really an Acquaintance? | 147 |
| Have You Ever Been Betrayed? | 151 |
| Do You Remember the Good Old Days? | 155 |
| 25 Ways to Screw Up Your Kids | 159 |
| A Message to Graduates: Here's the Best-Kept Secret | 163 |
| If You Had Three Wishes, What Would They Be? | 167 |
| What's Your Personal Brand Worth? | 171 |
| To Be or Not to Be | 175 |
| Are You Rich or Do You Just Have Money? | 179 |
| Do You Spend More Time Giving or Taking? | 183 |
| It's Time for Grown-Ups to Grow Up | 187 |
| You Can Do Better | 191 |
| Who's Your Role Model? | 195 |
| A Simple Reminder That Could Change Your Life | 199 |

**IMPOSSIBLE IS ALWAYS POSSIBLE**     **203**

## CHALLENGES      205

    Freedom and Personal Responsibility Go Hand in Hand    207
    The Glue That Supports a Healthy Social Fabric    211
    Ever Hear the Excuse "Everybody Does It"?    215

## CHANGE BEGINS WITH YOU      219

## RESOURCES      221

    35 Questions to Inspire Self-Reflection    223
    Why Do You Trust Some People and Mistrust Others?    227
    15 Common Habits of Mediocre People    231
    13 Mindsets That Might Be Holding You Back    235
    Do You Have a Big Head? You Be the Judge    239
    Are You Trying Too Hard to Please Everyone?    243
    How to Fight Complacency    247
    How to Give Feedback    251
    What Can Be More Important Than Your Cell Phone?    255
    You Get What You Expect    257
    My Best Advice    261

## ABOUT THE AUTHOR      267

## OTHER TITLES FROM FRANK SONNENBERG      269

# ACKNOWLEDGMENTS

Many people have asked me why I'm so passionate about *doing what's right* and how my personal philosophy came to be.

Although some people can point to one person, experience, or event that influenced their personal philosophy, I don't feel that applies to me. Instead, my views were shaped by a conscious effort to learn from many people and experiences throughout my life. I've been blessed by having excellent role models. They helped me appreciate the significance of strong moral character, personal values, personal responsibility and a strong family structure. They instilled the importance of having high expectations and the impact that a positive mental attitude could have on achieving those goals. They taught me the importance of a solid education, the value of continuous learning, and how personal experiences coupled with self-reflection could help shape my life.

As far back as I can remember, I've asked myself questions such as: How do people build trust and credibility? What makes a superior role model? What are the character traits of an effective leader? What's the difference between success and happiness? And I've made it my business to find out. Most importantly, I've learned that personal responsibility can't be delegated. Your life is determined by the sum of the choices that you make. It doesn't matter how other people view you if you can't face yourself each day. After all, you have to live with yourself for the rest of your life. My goal in writing *Listen to Your Conscience* is to share what I've learned and to prove that moral character is the DNA of success and happiness.

---

This book represents the contributions of many people to whom I am most grateful.

Caron Sonnenberg is my wife and best friend. She is the first person to read and comment on my work. Her observations are extremely valuable and insightful. Thank you, Caron, for your encouragement and patience and for acting as an incredible sounding board for ideas. Love doesn't have an expiration date. I'm still in love with you after 40 years.

Carrie Ralston, Simple Girl Design LLC, designed the cover and interior of this book. She also designs and supports my blog. Carrie is an exceptional designer and an incredible person to boot. I've worked with many designers throughout my career and Carrie is among the very best. I thank my lucky stars that our paths crossed, and I feel blessed that she is a member of our team. Thank you, Carrie, for your marvelous work, your friendship, and for just being you.

Kathy Dix is our proofreader extraordinaire. She reviews every word I write before it sees the light of day. Kathy is knowledgeable, caring, and extraordinary at her craft. I've worked with her for almost 15 years and she still continues to amaze me. Her insight is invaluable. Kathy, I appreciate you more than words can express.

Eric Wagner, Fifth Cup LLC, is the technology guru who keeps my blog humming along. Eric is knowledgeable and experienced and has a work ethic second to none. Eric does his magic, each day, so that I don't have to think about it. Eric, you make a tough job look easy. Thank you so much!

Now you've met the team. As I write these paragraphs I feel so blessed that I get to work with these folks each day. They're not only exceptional at their craft, they embody the principles depicted in this book.

---

As I was writing the introductory paragraph of the Acknowledgments section, I thought about people who've made an incredible difference in my life. Some folks showed me the ropes while others brought out the best in me or inspired me by being extraordinary role models. In any case, I thought it would be an interesting exercise to list 25 of them as a way of saying "Thank you" for being a special part of my life. (Of course, there are many others who could have been listed, but I limited the selection to 25.)

*My deepest gratitude.*

My list:

Martin Schwarzschild • Lynette Muller • Coach Richard Pond
Terry Shanley • Bernard Weissman • David Goldberg • Paul Crane
Ed Shulman • Gabriel Carlin • Alan Hembrough • Joseph Dattoli
John Sifonis • Mike Davidson • Michael E. Graupner • Tom Phillips
Tracy Benson • Beverly Goldberg • Marty Edelson • Bart Luedeke
Nancy Oliver Gray • Susan Christian • Sharon Telesca Feurer
Beverly Rath • Carrie Ralston • William Cosgrove

*YOU have the power to make a difference in someone's life.
These people made an incredible difference in mine!*

I'd like to shine the spotlight on other special people who have helped to shape my character and have contributed so much to making my life rewarding and meaningful.

One evening, decades ago, I was sitting on some steps in the college student center feeling sorry for myself. I had a statistics exam the next day, and it was going to be ugly. Mark Sandberg, PhD, my management professor (who later became the business college dean), saw me sulking. Mark approached me and asked if I wanted to grab a cup of coffee with him. The exchange didn't do much for the exam, but the friendship that resulted changed my life. After that encounter, I never made a major decision without consulting Mark first. There is a saying, "The mediocre teacher tells. The good teacher explains. The superior teacher demonstrates. The great teacher inspires." But what do you call the teacher who changes someone's life? Mark Sandberg.

I consider myself extremely blessed to have reported to Dave Tierno, former Senior Partner, Management Consulting Group, Ernst and Young, for over a decade. Dave was an incredibly effective leader, but what made Dave so special was *how* he achieved success. Some people talk about honor and integrity; others lead by example. It's been over 30 years since I worked for Dave. Yet whenever I have a hard time deciding what's *the right thing* to do, all I have to ask myself is, what would Dave do?

The first time I met Ed Berryman, I wondered if it's possible for any person to be so gifted, humble, and kind. Caron and I have become very good friends with Ed and his wife, Joanne. They represent all the goodness in the world. Moreover, we've gotten to know the rest of the Berryman clan quite well. The apple doesn't fall far from the tree.

The real determinant of success is not measured by great achievements but by the way you choose to wear it. Jody and Denis Salamone are humble, generous, and kind. They're family-oriented, give generously to their community, and have never forgotten their roots. Jody and Denis are extraordinary role models who lead by example every day. Caron and I are honored to call them good friends.

Larry Frankel is a good friend, a trusted confidant, and an outstanding role model. Larry grew up in humble beginnings and achieved tremendous success through sheer brilliance, hard work, and living with honor and integrity. When I define the characteristics of strong moral character, I'm describing Larry. He is proof positive that the American Dream is alive and well and that good people finish first.

My parents fled Germany during the Hitler years. They didn't complain about what life dealt them because they knew they were lucky to make it safely to America. Like many others, they loved this country and had hopes of building a good life for their family and living the American Dream.

My mother and father were wonderful role models who instilled the strong values in me that are so much a part of this book. My brothers and I grew up in a household where honesty and integrity presided over all else, where people's wealth was measured by their character rather than their material possessions, and where people got more joy from giving than from asking for more. They believed that we lived in the Land of Opportunity and that we could be anyone or do anything as long as we had the will and the desire to achieve our dreams.

Caron and I raised our girls, Catherine and Kristine, to be good people and to take great pleasure in life's journey. We're so proud of them. We're thrilled not only with what they've accomplished, but more importantly, with who they've become. They have strong moral character, wonderful values, and an incredible perspective about life. They're married to wonderful guys, Eric and John, who share their beliefs and principles and are really good souls. We're proud to call them our sons. It's fun for us to watch them raise their children. As I say, "Behind every good kid are parents who understand the importance of raising them that way." Catherine and Eric – Kristine and John – are determined to make a positive difference in the world. I'm sure they will!

Caron Sonnenberg is my wife and best friend. I feel so blessed with the life that we've lived. The best decision I ever made was to marry Caron. From the moment we met, we were inseparable. I knew she was the right one for me, but I never could have imagined the impact she would have on my life. We've been married for 40 years. And I can say that my life wouldn't be complete without her. I love Caron as much today as when we first met. I feel like the luckiest guy in the world – lucky that Caron and I said, "I do."

The world is a better place because of all these folks – mine certainly is!

And last but certainly not least, I'd like to give a shout-out to all the folks who read, comment, and share my blog posts each day. At the time of this book's publication, *FrankSonnenbergOnline* has an audience just shy of four million people. Together, we're making a difference. Thank YOU for helping me spread the word that moral character matters!

*Thank you all!*

"

FOLLOW YOUR
CONSCIENCE.
YOU HAVE TO LIVE
WITH YOURSELF
FOR THE REST
OF YOUR LIFE.

"

# INTRODUCTION

"

BE A GOOD PERSON.
EVERYTHING ELSE
IS SECONDARY.

"

# ARE YOU BLURRING THE DISTINCTION BETWEEN RIGHT AND WRONG?

What would happen if the line between right and wrong became blurred? Can you imagine a world in which cheating is acceptable, lying is tolerated, and stealing is a way of life? Imagine a world in which rules are ignored, laws are overlooked, and traditions are disregarded.

Can you imagine the stress and anxiety that would result if "every man for himself" became standard behavior? How about if people felt emboldened to speak their mind regardless of whether they offended others by being rude, disrespectful, or hurtful? That would change the way that you viewed relationships, treated business associates, and raised your children. Pretty ugly, right?

You may be thinking that this "Wild Wild West" scenario could never happen. Maybe so. But what would happen if the clear distinction between right and wrong became blurred? The result? Immoral behavior would become so prevalent it would alter our social fabric.

This could actually occur if people lowered their standards and closed their eyes to immorality and if there were no consequences for bad behavior. In that scenario, people could justify their actions by claiming that the end justifies the means and declaring that if "everybody does it," it must be acceptable. Right? Unfortunately, this mindset would send a strong signal that unacceptable conduct is now considered normal.

*Wrongs committed by enough people become the norm.*

## DO YOU KNOW RIGHT FROM WRONG?

If this scenario scares you, it should. If this nightmare ever came to pass, it wouldn't occur overnight. It would be the result of small acts flying under the radar – over a period of time.

When people say mean-spirited things in a joking manner, make personal attacks in a heated debate, and when mobs force their personal beliefs on others, the result is the same. We are blurring the distinction between right and wrong. The fact is, *actions* have consequences; *words* do, too. When bad behavior isn't challenged, it becomes acceptable to act in an unacceptable way.

Every time you excuse dishonesty, cover for misconduct, or fail to hold people accountable for their actions, you're complicit in dragging us down. Every time you're too uncomfortable to speak up or too busy to get involved, or you give someone a pass – because *you* benefit – you're bringing us one step closer to this nightmare scenario. Over time, norms collapse, traditions break down, and people become desensitized to immorality. Bad behavior becomes the new normal. If that occurs, it will be nearly impossible to raise good kids because they'll be surrounded by toxic people, bombarded by rotten entertainment, and besieged by negative role models. Is that what you want?

*Our future is dependent on our kids.*
*And the future of your children is dependent on you.*

You have the power to make a difference – if you try. Virtue isn't demanding more of others; it's expecting more of yourself. Be a good person. Everything else is secondary. Follow your conscience, be an exemplary role model, lead by example, and hold people accountable for their actions – even if it's uncomfortable to do so. While it's tough to change the world, you can change the world around you. There's a huge difference between right and wrong. It's our job to point out that reality to those who have forgotten.

Listen to your conscience. That's why you have one. :)

# LIFE LESSONS

> INNER PEACE IS A BYPRODUCT OF HOW YOU CHOOSE TO LIVE YOUR LIFE.

# INNER PEACE IS A CHOICE

What keeps you up at night? Maybe you regret something that you did or feel guilty about something that you failed to do. Perhaps it's because you haven't been honest with others or true to yourself. Or maybe your conscience is just trying to get your attention. In any case, have you ever wondered why some people are up all hours of the night, while others have peace of mind? The fact is, inner peace is a byproduct of how you choose to live your life.

Quite likely, your habits are so ingrained that you never think about your behavior or the many choices that you make. You choose to live in the moment or to dredge up your past, see the glass half-full or see it as half-empty, and live with honor or turn a blind eye to unethical behavior. Those habits have a significant impact on your psyche as well as on your general well-being.

*Peace of mind begins with the right mindset.*

## INNER PEACE — BE COOL, CALM, AND COLLECTED

If you're yearning for peace of mind, give these 15 guideposts some serious thought.

**Accept responsibility.** Be the master of your destiny rather than outsourcing your responsibility to others. Stand tall by accepting accountability for your choices and for the consequences of your actions.

**Find your purpose.** Make a difference. When you do something for satisfaction rather than reward, the reward is often the satisfaction of doing it.

**Live with honor.** Do what's right, not out of fear of getting caught, but because your integrity matters.

**Be reasonable.** Strive for excellence, not perfection. Excellence is more than sufficient.

**Develop trusting relationships.** Surround yourself with people who bring out the best in you. Gain their trust by proving that you're worthy of it.

**Make everyone a winner.** Focus on win-win relationships rather than on winner-take-all. Seek areas of common interest, where everyone can benefit, rather than on optimizing your individual situation.

**Be thankful.** Learn the meaning of *enough*. Find your happiness, not by seeking more, but by appreciating what you already have.

**Strive for balance.** Enjoy the journey as well as the destination. Happiness is not a matter of intensity but of balance.

**Learn to say "no."** Make your priorities a priority. Know what matters most to you and be unwilling to compromise those priorities at any price.

**Live in the moment.** Leave the past behind. You can't do anything to improve your past, but you can learn from it to improve your future.

**Unclutter your world.** Take a load off your mind. Don't allow fear, guilt, worry, envy, and anger to weigh you down.

**Control what you can.** Keep things in perspective. You can't control the uncontrollable, but you can control how you respond to it.

**Be true to yourself.** Reach for the stars and be proud of your achievements, but also take pride in the way that you achieve them.

**Build good karma.** Give of yourself, not because you expect something in return, but because witnessing others' happiness is, by itself, a worthy reward.

**Hold your head up high.** Make yourself proud. If you don't believe in yourself, why should anyone else?

*If you believe you can't…you won't.*

## FIND INNER PEACE

Some folks are wealthy, but their relationships are poor. They have a big title at work but aren't much of a Dad or Mom at home. They're successful, but everyone knows *how* they achieved that success. The truth is, some of those folks are self-centered, ruthless, and unapologetic – and they know it. Maybe that's why they're not sleeping.

Inner peace isn't just the ability to deal with conflict; it's knowing full well that you're a person of honor and integrity. It's knowing that you do the right thing, serve as an exemplary role model, and make a difference in the lives of others. That enables you to hold your head up high and to sleep well at night. Marvin Gaye of Motown fame once said, "If you cannot find peace within yourself, you will never find it anywhere else." What some folks overlook in their quest for power, fame, and fortune is that following your conscience, and having inner peace, clearly outweighs the material rewards received along the way. After all, you have to live with yourself for the rest of your life. :)

"

YOU HAVE THE FREEDOM TO CHOOSE, BUT YOU'RE NOT FREE FROM THE CONSEQUENCES OF THOSE CHOICES.

"

# TAKE OWNERSHIP BY TAKING RESPONSIBILITY

You have choices. You can live a healthy lifestyle or eat to your heart's content. You can spend money like a drunken sailor or invest in your future. You can listen to your conscience or fall victim to temptation. The fact is, you have the freedom to choose, but you're not free from the consequences of those choices. That's *your* responsibility.

Some folks, however, never learn that valuable lesson. In fact, they don't spend much time at all thinking about consequences. It's probably because they've become whizzes at dodging their responsibility, or they don't see *immediate* fallout resulting from their behavior.

*Choices are easy. The tough part is living with them.*

## WHY RESPONSIBILITY MATTERS

When things go well, it's awesome; when they don't…oh well. The question is, do you accept responsibility for your actions, learn from the experience, and move on? Or do you go into denial, sweep the problem under the rug, and find someone else to blame?

You can't take control of your life until you're accountable for your behavior and the choices that you make. When you dodge responsibility, you spend more time inventing excuses than trying to right the ship. When actions don't have consequences, there's no reason to work hard; there's no incentive to be determined; and there's no motivation to up your game. That can cause you to get lazy, sloppy, and stale. Ouch!

## IF YOU'RE NOT RESPONSIBLE FOR YOUR ACTIONS, WHO IS?

Own your choices rather than relinquishing that responsibility to others. Determine who you want to be; set the direction you wish to take; and focus your efforts on your goals. When you own your life, you choose to:

**Accept yourself and your circumstances** rather than feeling powerless and helpless, unable to affect the outcome.

**Abide by your beliefs and values** rather than allowing yourself to be bullied by peer pressure and persuaded to follow the pack.

**Pursue your inner peace** rather than seeking acceptance from others.

**Face challenges with courage and conviction** rather than surrendering your dreams to fear.

**Openly acknowledge mistakes** rather than finding a scapegoat.

**Control your thoughts and emotions** rather than allowing anger, fear, guilt, or envy to get the better of you.

**Live every day to the fullest** rather than becoming trapped by reliving disappointments of the past.

**Accept ownership of your health and emotional well-being** rather than submitting to self-defeating behavior.

**Follow your conscience** rather than selling your soul to the highest bidder.

**Believe in yourself** rather than measuring your self-worth based on what others think of you.

## IT'S YOUR RESPONSIBILITY — AND YOURS ALONE

Our society has standards of acceptable behavior. But the rules of decency are meaningless if there aren't any consequences. When parents overlook bad behavior, when leaders look the other way, when citizens let their conscience hibernate, it's easy to become desensitized to poor behavior. So, while you may think you're doing someone a favor by giving them a free pass, it's a recipe for disaster. The fact is, when you don't face consequences, there are consequences for that, too.

*Don't look to others; look to yourself.*

Personal responsibility needn't be a burden. It's a blessing to own your life. Be the master of your destiny with a vested interest in your actions. Take pride in who you are and what you do. Stand tall by taking charge rather than outsourcing your responsibility to others. Accountability can't be delegated. If you look in the mirror and don't like what you see, don't blame the mirror. It can't be done *for you*; it must be done *by you*. :)

"

PEOPLE CAN'T MAKE YOU DO THINGS WITHOUT YOUR PERMISSION.

"

# NEVER LOWER YOUR PERSONAL STANDARDS. NEVER!

When you go into a room, your body adapts to the temperature. The same holds true for your mindset. How much are you influenced by the people you spend time with? Do they bring out the best in you? Or do you find yourself compromising your values, mimicking improper behavior, or lowering your personal standards?

While it may be tempting to take the easy route, to follow the crowd, or to be seduced by riches, *you* are responsible for your conduct – and the consequences of your actions – regardless of how others behave.

*People can't make you do things without your permission.*

## YOUR PERSONAL STANDARDS DEFINE YOU

Never lower your standards, compromise your integrity, or dishonor your name. Here are 10 ways people degrade themselves:

**Give in to temptation.** Some folks stretch the truth, let their eyes wander, or get seduced by money. I hope you have the willpower and self-respect to say "no."

**Relax their standards.** Some people are tempted to lower their standards because others are slacking off. While it may be appealing to take a breather, bad habits are hard to break.

**Follow the crowd.** Some folks follow the pack because they assume others know better. Even though a group may provide comfort and security, it doesn't guarantee that their motives are pure or that they're thinking rationally or ethically. Know when to say "no."

**Mimic inappropriate behavior.** Some people fall into a bad crowd and imitate their behavior. The truth is, "Everybody does it" doesn't mean *you* have to do it.

**Look the other way.** Some folks turn their backs, fail to speak out, or cover up for unethical behavior because it's convenient. Every time you close your eyes to immorality or injustice, you're condoning it.

**Crave acceptance.** Some people will do *anything* to win acceptance from the in-crowd. Think long and hard before you pay the price of admission.

**Get dragged into a tussle.** Some people always seem to be looking for a fight. While you may be provoked to jump in, think twice before you take the plunge. As a famous saying goes, "Never wrestle with pigs. You both get dirty and the pig likes it."

**Lose control of their temper.** Some folks respond emotionally, which is never a good idea. If you're angry or upset, count to 10 before communicating your feelings. If that doesn't work, try 20.

**Compromise their values.** Some folks impose their way of thinking on others. You win a debate with a better argument, not by force.

**Take shortcuts.** Some folks act unethically to look good, cover their behind, or get what they want. The prize for living with honor and integrity is that, even though you won't win all the time, you'll be true to yourself and your values.

## RAISE YOUR PERSONAL STANDARDS

Jim Rohn, author and entrepreneur, famously said, "You're the average of the five people you spend the most time with." What he's saying is that people will influence you. It's only natural. That being said, I hope you spend time with folks who are smart, kind, and honorable – but what if they're not?

Be aware of the impact that others have on your behavior. Don't let bad habits, weak character, low standards, or immoral behavior rub off on you. If anything, be a positive influence on others and an inspiration to them.

> *Keeping bad company is like being in a germ-infested area.*
> *You never know what you'll catch.*

Be your own person. Set your bar high and don't lower your standards for anyone. You're better than that. Some of the most precious things you possess are your honor, your dignity, and your reputation. Be the person others look up to – whose character is beyond reproach. Be the one who inspires others to achieve excellence. And be the one who lives with honor and dignity. At the end of the day, if you're not proud of who you are and the way you choose to live your life, little else matters.  :)

"

SITUATIONS ARE RARELY BLACK OR WHITE; THE TRUTH LIES SOMEWHERE IN-BETWEEN.

"

# IS YOUR GLASS HALF-FULL OR HALF-EMPTY?

Do your days ever start off crappy? Your kid has a cold, you run into heavy traffic on your way to work, and the milk in your coffee is sour. Really? If it's not one thing, it's another. You get cut off by a driver, your computer goes on the fritz, or your favorite shirt gets stained. Sound familiar? None of these problems is so monumental that you'd step out onto a ledge, but some people still go to extremes by saying, "My life sucks!"

Some people can accept nuisances in the normal course of events while others go off the rails and think the world is coming to an end. Of course, you have the right to get upset when bad things happen. But negativity, in general, can be counterproductive – especially when you allow negative thoughts to spiral out of control. That kind of behavior not only puts you in a bad mood, it can undermine all of the positive things that you do.

## IS YOUR GLASS HALF-FULL OR HALF-EMPTY?

Do you see the glass as half-full or half-empty? Although both ways of looking at things are technically correct, your perspective can have a huge impact on your success and happiness.

**Happiness.** When you continually see the glass as half-empty, you may convince yourself that you're having a bad day, even when you're not. So if you *don't* want to put yourself in a lousy mood, stop being negative and making yourself feel bad.

*If you ignore a negative thought,
it may be replaced by a positive one.*

**Success.** Negative thoughts can turn into self-fulfilling prophecies. When you expect a bad outcome, you look for evidence to support that view. Your expectations can have a significant impact on results.

If you don't believe that's true, think of the impact that a placebo can have on your health. The placebo effect is an amazing phenomenon in which some people experience a beneficial health outcome after the administration of a "fake" treatment, simply because they *believe* it will make them better. Give that some thought next time you think, "I'm doomed from the start" or "People like me don't stand a chance."

## LOOK ON THE BRIGHT SIDE

A positive mental attitude can improve your health, enhance your relationships, increase your chances of success, and add years to your life. What can you do to change your mindset? Here are seven places to start:

**Get real.** Things happen. Get over it. Even if life were a bed of roses, you'd still need to avoid the thorns.

**See it from a different angle.** Situations are rarely black or white; the truth lies somewhere in-between.

**Keep things in perspective.** Don't blow things out of proportion and make a mountain out of a molehill.

**Stop feeling sorry for yourself.** If you can't make it better, don't make it worse by being negative. Whenever you think you have it bad, you find someone else who has it worse.

**Be nice.** Some people are nicer to friends than they are to themselves. When you say, "I'm such an idiot," "I can't do anything right," or "I'm such a loser," you undermine your self-worth and confidence.

**Break the habit.** Are you filling your head with empty calories? Stop complaining. It won't solve anything. It'll only drag you down.

**Fake it.** Be conscious of your thoughts and try to see the bright side. As Dale Carnegie said, "Act enthusiastic and you will be enthusiastic."

## PEP TALK OR DEBBIE DOWNER?

When crowds of people cheer you on during a marathon, it can have a tremendous impact on your performance. That's true in sports and in daily life. So be your own cheerleader!

It's your choice whether to view the glass as half-full or half-empty. My advice is to make every effort to be positive. Start today! Don't dip your toe in the water. Jump in with both feet. It'll have a huge impact on your health and happiness. Don't wait for someone to do it for you. Make the effort yourself. As the saying goes, "You can lead a horse to water, but you can't make him drink."  :)

"

PEOPLE CHANGE
ONLY WHEN CHANGE
IS THEIR CHOICE.

"

# ARE YOU INFLEXIBLE AND STUCK IN YOUR WAYS?

A category 4 hurricane can pack winds of up to 156 miles per hour. Why do palm trees that stretch to the sky often survive hurricane-force winds, while well-built frame houses give way like toothpicks? The fact is, the houses are rigid and take the lashing head-on, while the palm trees are flexible and can bend to the ground. Do you adapt to your environment or are you stuck in your ways?

The world is changing at a blistering rate. Are you *willing* to change with the times or are you rigid and set in your ways? Think about how your mindset may be helping or hurting your efforts.

*Excuses proclaim an unwillingness to change.*

## ARE YOU FLEXIBLE OR RIGID?

Use the following 25 strategies to identify whether your habits are propelling you forward or holding you back.

**Roll with the punches.** Expect the unexpected. Ready or not, the future will happen.

**Get real.** Accept reality for what it is – not for what you want it to be.

**Be positive.** Do you see the glass as half-full or half-empty? Make your outlook work *for* rather than *against* you. Your mindset matters more than you think.

**Challenge your routines.** Are you open to change? "I can't" and "I don't want to" trigger the same results.

**Be realistic.** You can't control the uncontrollable, but you can control how you respond to those situations.

**Face your fears.** Face your challenges head-on rather than surrendering your dreams to fear. If you don't *try*, you forfeit the opportunity.

**Learn from mistakes.** Do you repeat mistakes? Make experience your best teacher. Lessons in life will be repeated until they are learned.

**Let go of your anger.** Do you harbor anger and resentment? Forgiving doesn't mean forgetting, nor does it mean approving of, what someone did. It just means that you're letting go of the anger toward that person.

**End the bad relationship.** Toxic waste has a tremendous impact on the environment. Consider the impact that toxic people have on your life.

**Know what matters most.** Are your priorities in order? The more you say "no" to things that don't matter, the more time you have for things that do.

**Keep an open mind.** Do you listen to differing viewpoints? Try to see their side of the issue. You just may learn something.

**Leave a bad work situation.** If work isn't fun, you're playing on the wrong team.

**Learn something new.** Are you a know-it-all? Unless you learn something new every day, you're becoming obsolete.

**Simplify your life.** Your life is as complicated as you make it.

**Stop overthinking everything.** Once you've made your decision, don't look back. Make it work.

**Live within your means.** When you run out of money, stop buying.

**Be kind to yourself.** Do you judge, criticize, or find fault with yourself? Be your own best friend.

**Give up control.** If you can't change the outcome, move on to an area within your control.

**Make *yourself* proud.** When you constantly seek approval, you give more weight to another person's opinion than to your own.

**Enlist support.** Do you try to do everything yourself? Have faith in others. Learn how to delegate.

**Just say "no."** When you're hijacked by other people's priorities, you don't have time to tackle your own. Make *your* priorities a priority.

**Manage your expectations.** Strive for excellence rather than perfection.

**Admit fault.** Are you too proud to apologize? The two greatest time-savers are saying "I don't know" and "I was wrong."

**Know when to quit.** If you reach a dead end, it may be time to stop.

**Live with honor.** Everything has a price, but *not* everything should be for sale. Listen to your conscience. That's why you have one.

## PEOPLE CHANGE ONLY WHEN CHANGE IS THEIR CHOICE

Although your habits have served you in the past, that may not be true today. The reality is, applying old formulas to new world problems doesn't add up. If you're using a hammer when the job requires a screwdriver, you're going to face troubled times ahead. Therefore, don't wait for storm clouds to appear before you act. Embrace change while the sun is still shining. :)

"

TRUST IS LIKE LOVE.
IT CAN'T BE SEEN,
BUT ITS VALUE IS
IMMEASURABLE.

"

# DO YOU DESERVE TO BE TRUSTED?

Some things occur naturally, like the sunrise, seasons, and the changing of the tides. Many folks put *trust* in the same category, thinking it's simply a natural outgrowth of relationships. Nothing could be further from the truth. What's more, if you believe that trust is inevitable, you're far less likely to make the effort required to earn it. Do you deserve to be trusted?

Even though most people acknowledge the importance of trust, there's no easy way to gauge its progress. In fact, you're probably unaware that you constantly evaluate people's trustworthiness, but you actually do. Think of it as a mental scorecard. You give folks a nod of approval every time they prove worthy of your trust. And you become wary of them every time they disappoint you.

> *You've never given something so much thought,*
> *without really thinking.*

When someone displays *ethical behavior* on a *consistent* basis, you're able to predict *future* conduct with some degree of *confidence*. BUT, if inappropriate behavior is displayed at any time during the process, it'll cast a shadow on the relationship. And you may even question whether you should trust that person.

*Trust takes a long time to develop,
but it can be lost in the blink of an eye.*

## 15 WAYS YOU DETERMINE IF SOMEONE SHOULD BE TRUSTED

Think about why you trust some people and not others. What is it about their behavior that makes you trust them?

Do these thoughts cross your mind:

> "I can always count on him. He'd never let me down."

> "She's the same person in public as she is in private."

> "His promise is as good as a contract."

> "She's always willing to help others and rarely asks for anything in return."

> "He tells me the truth – even when it hurts."

> "She'd never say anything behind my back that she wouldn't say directly to me."

> "He treats everyone warmly – even if they can't do anything for him."

> "She doesn't spin the truth. She tells it like it is."

> "He's always on time. I can set my watch by him."

> "She has strong convictions. She doesn't blow in the wind."

> "He's respectful, even when he doesn't agree with me."

> "She'd never ask me to do anything that she wouldn't do herself."

"He's a good friend. I can count on him in good times and bad."

"She's very fair – open-minded, objective, and even-handed."

"I never fear that he's withholding information from me."

This list represents a few considerations involved in determining whether or not to trust someone. Many factors come into play, including honesty, integrity, dependability, reliability, compassion, selflessness, authenticity, fairness, tolerance, humility, kindness, forgiveness, loyalty, commitment, and transparency.

The fact is, trusting someone is a personal decision in which everyone employs a different rating scale – giving more weight to some factors than to others. In addition, you're not the only one judging people based on these factors; they're judging you as well.

## ARE YOU WORTHY OF TRUST?

Trust is *not* granted because you possess power, wealth, or status. Similarly, trust isn't given because you demand or desire it. When someone places their trust in you, you've proven that you're worthy of their trust and that you'll work hard to preserve it.

All it takes is money to buy a gift, but when you grant someone trust, it's a gift from your heart. When you place your faith in someone, you're inviting them to join an exclusive group. After all, you're indicating that they have met your moral standards and you'd be honored to forge a very special relationship with them. From this moment forward, you will place your trust in the palms of their hands, knowing that it will be treated with care. What's that worth? Trust is like love. It can't be seen, but its value is immeasurable. :)

"

THERE'S NO SUCH THING AS TRUST AT FIRST SIGHT.

"

# 15 COMMON MYTHS ABOUT BUILDING TRUST

A **sound reputation *always* leads to trust.** A reputation is helpful in building trust, but it's only a start. Most people validate your reputation by comparing it to their actual experience with you. If your reputation matches their experience, you're home free. If not, building trust may be an uphill climb.

**Trust doesn't *always* have to be earned.** Some folks believe that having power, wealth, or status entitles them to be trusted. Nothing could be further from the truth. Trust is earned.

**Trust can't be rushed.** There's no such thing as trust at first sight. People will test you in small ways before trusting you outright. Trust is built when *honorable* behavior is *consistently* performed, *over a period of time*. When your honorable conduct becomes *predictable*, *faith* – the highest level of trust – is born.

**Talking a good game leads to trust.** You send a message by what you say and what you do. If your words aren't supported with consistent actions, they will ring hollow.

**Trust exists between two people.** True. But if you're hurtful to someone (and the word gets out), others may think that if you did it to someone else, it "might be me one day."

**You either trust someone or you don't.** Trust isn't an either/or proposition — it falls somewhere along a continuum. Trust is based on factors such as honesty, integrity, fairness, reliability, dependability, and transparency in a relationship. In addition, there are different degrees of trust. While you might trust a customer service employee to help you with a problem, you might not trust that individual to manage your finances or care for your children.

**We all develop trust the same way.** Prior relationships and personal bias may influence the way you view and/or develop trust. For example, if you believe that people are trustworthy, you'll probably manage relationships differently than if you think people are out to get you.

**It's acceptable to break *small* promises, but not *big* ones.** Some people believe that it's acceptable to break small promises. That's simply not true. For example, if you continually show up late, people may wonder — if they can't count on you to be timely, can they depend on you in general?

**All mistakes produce *equal* damage to a relationship.** There are two kinds of mistakes, *accidental* and *intentional*. Despite our best efforts, there's nothing we can do to prevent accidents, as they are by their very nature out of our control. The second type of mistake, however, is deliberate. Intentional acts weaken trust.

*A deliberate mistake is* not *the same as an accidental one.*

**Breaching trust always kills a relationship.** For the most part, people are forgiving if you make an honest mistake or act out of character on occasion. But when improper actions — such as lying, cheating, or stealing — are repeated, it can significantly impact your relationship.

**Once an apology is made, all is forgiven.** An apology should be heartfelt – rather than an attempt to smooth ruffled feathers. But even if you offer a heartfelt apology, it may still require time and effort to reestablish trust. Moreover, if you repeat the act, you're indicating that you were more interested in creating peace than in changing your ways.

**If I trust someone, you'll probably trust him too.** Building trust is personal. Just because *you* have a trusting relationship with someone doesn't guarantee that I will.

**Trust lasts forever.** Trust takes a long time to develop, but it can be lost in the blink of an eye.

**Repairing trust requires the same effort as building it.** It takes a lot *more* effort to rebuild trust than to establish it from the start. Therefore, think twice before you act. As the saying goes, "You can't unring a bell."

**Everyone stands an equal chance of securing trust.** Some people find it easier to build trust than others do. Why? you ask. They set high standards of behavior and adhere to them. They prove that they're worthy of your trust instead of thinking that trust occurs by magic. There is *magic* in trust. But earning it requires more than *illusion*. :)

"

# ARE YOU HONORABLE OR AFRAID OF GETTING CAUGHT?

"

# WOULD YOU DO SOMETHING UNETHICAL IF YOU COULD GET AWAY WITH IT?

Lying, cheating, stealing. I assume you know the difference between right and wrong. The question is whether you abstain from those acts because you're honorable or because you're afraid of getting caught. Would you do something unethical if you could get away with it?

Nobody, except the perpetrator, really knows why an unscrupulous act was committed. If *you* were the perpetrator, were you taking a shortcut, covering up the truth, scamming the system, giving in to a moment of weakness, or selling your soul to the devil? Regardless of the reason, the result is the same – even though *others may not know* that you committed the act, you'll know for sure. And you have to live with that fact.

How does that make you feel? While some people would feel guilty, dirty, or even worthless, others are oblivious. For them, it's all about the prize.

## ARE YOU HONORABLE OR AFRAID OF GETTING CAUGHT?

We are regularly faced with choices that fall in the gray area of moral behavior. Other times, our choices are clear as day. The truth is that selective morality is sinful. Determine if the following 15 points are clear in your mind.

Is stealing someone else's idea as dishonest as stealing a possession?

If you do something unscrupulous, *to benefit others*, does that make it right?

If your boss tells you to do something unethical, does that excuse immoral behavior?

Is stealing the credit that belongs to someone else really stealing?

Is overlooking dishonest behavior as bad as committing the act?

Are you a winner if you cheat?

Does talking about morality make you a good person?

Is spreading lies as cruel as creating them?

If you fail to report dishonest behavior, are you being dishonest?

Is telling a "white lie" lying?

Is omitting a key fact as bad as telling a blatant lie?

Is breaking a small commitment as bad as breaking a large one?

If several others commit a wrongdoing, is it appropriate to copy them?

Does the size of a reward ever justify shady behavior?

Is stealing a little as bad as stealing a lot?

## WHAT IS YOUR DIGNITY WORTH TO YOU?

You're going to be tested throughout your life. You may be tempted to cheat to make yourself look good, stretch the truth to cover your behind, or do something unethical to get what you want. The challenge is that the *right choice* might not always be as clear as day. That's when your actions reveal your true character.

It's easy to say what you'll do in theory, but your actions count most when the rubber meets the road. Your choice is clear. Will you live a life that makes you proud or choose a path of dishonor and deceit?

To make matters more complicated, your answer may not always be on full display. In fact, it may be a test in which *you* grade your own exam. No one will know how you performed – but you will.

*Is your conscience giving you the silent treatment?*

If you choose the path of honor and integrity, there may be some negative consequences. In fact, you may fall short of the prize that you had your heart set on; you may be forced to tell your boss you're not comfortable with his or her request; or, if you did something wrong, you may have some explaining to do.

The prize for being honest is that, even though you may not win all the time, you'll be true to yourself and your values. What's that worth? Everything! John Wooden, the legendary basketball coach, said, "The true test of a man's character is what he does when no one is watching." Would you do something unethical if you could get away with it? Follow your conscience. You have to live with yourself for the rest of your life.  :)

"

**BEING DISHONEST ISN'T AN INNOCENT MISTAKE — IT'S A DELIBERATE ACT TO DECEIVE.**

"

# EVER FEEL LIKE YOU'VE BEEN TAKEN?

Ever feel like you've been taken? Did you ever shop for something and feel so dirty during the buying process that you felt you needed to take a shower afterward? Even though you were pleased with the product, you felt that the buying experience was so sleazy it made your skin crawl.

What caused your unpleasant reaction? What can an organization do to avoid treating its customers this way?

## WHAT'S TURNING CUSTOMERS OFF?

In today's competitive business environment, it's important that business leaders take a few minutes to consider the following. Are you or your organization guilty of any of these 12 actions (or inactions)?

**Appearances.** If your office decor is dated, your customer may wonder whether your recommendations will be behind the times.

**Understanding customer needs.** If you're giving a boilerplate sales pitch, your customer may wonder whether your organization really cares about *their specific* needs.

**Pride.** If your emails contain typos, your customer may wonder – if you're too lazy to run spell-check, what other details are being overlooked?

**Responsiveness.** If your employee doesn't respond to emails promptly, your customer may wonder if you'll make yourselves available when they have a problem.

**Reliability.** If your employee is late for meetings, your customer may wonder whether your organization can be trusted to finish the job on time and within budget.

**Dependability.** If your employee cancels a scheduled meeting, your customer may wonder if you value other customers more than you value them.

**Competence.** If your salespeople can't answer basic product questions, your customer may wonder – if you hire mediocre people, could your product be any good?

**Courtesy.** If your employee doesn't know the consumer after all these years, your customer may wonder if you'll take their business for granted.

**Security.** If your employee's appearance is disheveled and his papers are sloppy, your customer may wonder whether their personal information is safe and secure.

**Access.** If your employee is impossible to get in touch with *before* the sale, your customer may wonder how they'll be treated *after* the sale.

**Communication.** If your customer learns about a policy change before hearing it *directly* from your employee, they may wonder whether the right hand knows what the left hand is doing.

**Commitment.** If your organization has excessive turnover, your customer may wonder what your employees know that they don't.

## AVOID THESE ACTIONS AT ALL COSTS

You undoubtedly recognize the damage that the preceding factors can have on your business! They can weaken any customer relationship. BUT those activities pale in comparison to the destruction caused by even the *appearance* of deception and dishonesty. The truth is, some items on the previous list can be attributed to stupidity or incompetence, but being dishonest isn't an innocent mistake – it's a deliberate act to deceive.

Here are 11 actions that are more than turnoffs. These actions will make your customers feel like they're being taken – and you may face legal problems. Avoid the following at all costs:

1. Deceiving the customer through bait-and-switch tactics.
2. Applying extreme pressure to force a hasty decision.
3. Distorting or exaggerating the truth in order to deceive.
4. Communicating in a haphazard manner to throw the customer off balance.
5. Withholding or omitting key information to intentionally mislead.
6. Burying details in the fine print to hide unfavorable information.
7. Breaking promises or commitments to benefit yourself.
8. Passing the buck and deflecting blame to avoid accountability.
9. Presenting unfinished work as complete.
10. Changing the terms of the agreement after an understanding is reached.
11. Being *unwilling* or *unable* to provide support after the sale is made.

*Anybody who says, "I didn't mean to lie" is being dishonest.*

## A CUSTOMER FOR LIFE

Many businesses view a sale as an isolated event, rather than as a long-term relationship with a customer. They believe that if a transaction is handled poorly, the cost is merely the loss of a single sale. Nothing could be further from the truth. You may lose the customer forever.

When you're in front of a customer, you may think you're only selling a product, but that's rarely the case. A long-term relationship hinges on trust and credibility. That doesn't happen by short-changing the customer. Everything you say and do will strengthen or weaken the bond of trust. The next time you're selling a product, remember that customers expect more than merchandise; they want to buy from a person they can count on and an organization they can trust. Character matters! :)

"

CREDIBILITY SAYS
EVERYTHING
ABOUT YOU.

"

# HOW CREDIBLE ARE YOU?

What do offering parental advice, applying for a job, or running for President have in common? It doesn't matter whether you're peddling a product, selling an idea, persuading a skeptical group, teaching your kids a life lesson, or leading people in times of uncertainty – you won't be successful if you lack trust and credibility.

*Credibility matters. Believe me!*

Credibility isn't automatic. You must prove that you're worthy of it. But beware! Once credibility is granted, it's not always permanent. Some folks undermine their efforts by disregarding the connection between their behavior and credibility. Others are so blinded by ambition that they're willing to sacrifice everything to get what they want. While that strategy may work in the short term, the impact on trust and credibility can be lasting.

*When you exaggerate a story, you weaken your credibility.*

## HOW TO EARN CREDIBILITY

Here are 14 factors that contribute to your credibility:

**Be genuine.** Credible people are comfortable in their own skin. They don't create a false persona to win acceptance, and they don't allow themselves to be manipulated by others.

**Be principled.** Credible people do what's right rather than what's convenient. They don't twist rules for personal gain.

**Be capable.** Credible people have a proven track record of success. Plus, they have the knowledge and experience to replicate that success. They don't misrepresent their capabilities to get something they don't deserve.

**Be discerning.** Credible people surround themselves with folks who uphold high standards of honor and integrity. They don't let toxic people pollute their attitude, dampen their drive, or corrupt their morality.

**Be honest and trustworthy.** Credible people give explanations in a *clear* and *concise* manner. They tell it *like it is* rather than saying what folks want to hear. They don't spin the truth or exaggerate benefits to make something sound better.

**Be straightforward and transparent.** Credible people let others know whether they're presenting fact or opinion. They don't abuse people's trust by making a recommendation or offering advice without revealing vested interests.

**Be objective.** Credible people present both sides of an issue rather than a one-sided view. They disclose all known facts in an unbiased manner and let recipients arrive at their own conclusion. They don't manipulate, suppress, or withhold important information to misrepresent the truth.

**Be selfless.** Credible people focus on win-win relationships rather than trying to advance their own self-interests. They don't try to win at the expense of the relationship.

**Be fair.** Credible people make every effort to be open-minded, even-handed, and non-discriminating. They don't show favoritism – rather, they treat superiors and subordinates with the same level of respect.

**Be rational and insightful.** Credible people examine both sides of an issue before forming an opinion. They make decisions based on hard evidence and reason rather than on emotion.

**Be virtuous.** Credible people are passionate about their beliefs and values. But they don't force them on others. They recognize that one of the true tests of integrity is your refusal to compromise your honor at any price.

**Be decisive and action-oriented.** Credible people don't just talk a good game – they make things happen. They jump on good opportunities, knowing full well that if you do nothing, nothing happens.

**Be accountable.** Credible people take ownership of their life rather than relinquishing that responsibility to others. They don't point a finger or cast blame to evade accountability.

**Be consistent and dependable.** Credible people are predictable. You always know where they stand. They don't blow with the wind, even when it's convenient and tempting to do so.

## CREDIBILITY SAYS EVERYTHING ABOUT YOU

Credibility is gauged by the level of confidence and trust that people have in you. You don't secure that by sharpening your resume, learning how to play-act, or giving yourself a makeover. You gain people's trust based on your moral character and your competence, and by consistently displaying admirable behavior.

*The truth never lies.*

Some people have it backward – they focus on how they *appear* to others. The truth is that credibility begins with you! If YOU don't believe in yourself, why should others? When you continually invest in your personal growth, live with honor, and lead by example, everything you say will carry the voice of credibility. Moreover, you'll be proud of who you are. You won't have to shout it from the rooftops; saying nothing will say everything. Are you credible? :)

"

KINDNESS IS THE
ONE GIFT THAT
YOU CAN KEEP
ON GIVING.

"

# WHAT DOES IT TAKE TO BE KIND?

Did you ever say "Good morning" to a stranger and have them look at you as if you were crazy? Sure...they may have been deep in thought or mulling over a personal problem, but was your greeting that unusual to warrant the reaction you received? What does it say about that person, much less about the world at large? Is being kind so uncommon that "Good morning" can make someone feel uncomfortable? Or is a simple act of kindness one of those things that we need more of today?

*Kindness is the one gift that you can keep on giving.*

## A SIMPLE ACT OF KINDNESS CAN GO A LONG WAY

For some folks, being kind is second nature, while for others it's a chore. You have to wonder why some people go out of their way to be mean. After all, being kind doesn't require any more effort than being cold and callous does. But some people seem to prefer it that way. They're either too darn busy, too self-absorbed, or can't be bothered to make the effort.

*No one has the right to be rude.*

In reality, being kind is a mindset more than an activity – you put others first rather than making everything about yourself. Consider some of the ways to show that you care:

> You can remember someone's name, call for no reason, lend an ear, give a compliment, hold the door open, give up your seat, give your undivided attention, remember a special occasion, steer the conversation to your companion, answer an email promptly, show someone the ropes, let someone go first, share the credit, write a thank-you note, pass on something of interest, or simply smile.

The possibilities are endless. As Aesop said, "No act of kindness, no matter how small, is ever wasted."

*Being kind is so easy, yet some folks make it seem so hard.*

## THE BENEFITS OF BEING KIND

Being kind will do as much for you as for the recipient. Here are 10 benefits of being kind:

**Make someone's day.** Take satisfaction in knowing that you put a smile on someone's face.

**Develop good habits.** When you look for opportunities to be kind, you force yourself to see the good in the world.

**Enhance your self-esteem.** Being kind makes you feel good about yourself.

**Forget your woes.** Instead of obsessing over your own problems, shift your focus toward others. You'll earn karma points in the process.

**Build stronger relationships.** Being kind helps to build stronger relationships because people tend to mirror the treatment they receive from you.

**Be a role model.** Take pride in knowing that you're a positive role model and that others may emulate your behavior.

**Improve your health.** Reduce stress and anxiety, improve heart health, and even increase your lifespan by being a kind and caring person.

**Enhance your success.** Being kind will come back to you in spades – because people gravitate to those who are positive and caring.

**Make a difference.** Know that you're making the world a better place one act of kindness at a time.

**Pay it forward.** Others will likely pay your benevolence forward. After all, kindness is contagious.

## BE ONE OF A KIND

Being kind and compassionate shouldn't be something that you're coerced into doing. It also shouldn't be about fulfilling an obligation or relieving guilt by writing a fat check.

Kindness should come from your heart and be given freely. What's more, if you give of yourself because you feel obliged, you lose something very special: the satisfaction of knowing that you're *willfully* making a difference – even if it's in a small way.

> *You don't have to be rich to give;*
> *your gift can be as simple as a smile.*

If you think we need more kindness in the world, you're not alone. But compassion isn't something that you can demand or shame others into giving; the best way to encourage kindness is to lead by example. So stand up and be counted. The fact is, an act of kindness may take only a minute, but its impact can be lasting.  :)

"
**IF YOU REWARD PEOPLE FOR NOTHING, WHY EXPECT ANYTHING?**
"

# ARE YOU HELPING PEOPLE BECOME HELPLESS?

Sometimes, well-intentioned plans have unintended consequences. We impose a mandatory gratuity so the server doesn't get stiffed; we let the mediocre employees "skate" because they're the breadwinners for their families; we say "yes" to our kids because we're their parents and we want them to be happy.

Even though our efforts may help the recipients in the short term, we are making them dependent on our good graces rather than preparing them to accept personal responsibility for their future. Here are some examples that occur every day:

> **Guaranteed gratuities.** Restaurant servers receive a 10% – 20% tip, regardless of the service they provide. This teaches servers that half-hearted work still gets rewarded. So why try harder? Their complacency ultimately hurts the restaurant because a superior customer experience is built on the establishment's ambiance, food, *and* service.
>
> **Automatic rewards.** Annual bonuses are sometimes based on employee tenure or "just showing up" rather than on merit. The fact is that people stop trying when there's no benefit for being exceptional and no consequence for being mediocre.

**Gifts of graduation.** Students are promoted to the next grade level regardless of whether they've met the minimum requirements. This "easy path" through school will surely catch up with the students one day.

**Better safe than sorry.** Safe spaces protect students from people who say or do things that may offend or make a student *feel* uncomfortable (regardless of whether there was any intent by the offender). Safe spaces denigrate the educational experience by limiting dissenting viewpoints, discouraging students from thinking for themselves, and making the whole campus community paranoid – fearing that they could be called out by an accuser.

**"Yes" – the most common cop-out.** When we say "yes" to kids merely to placate them, or avoid a scene in public, they never learn the difference between right and wrong. Saying "no" to your children, when appropriate, is an act of love.

**Unqualified quotas.** If opportunity is based on special quotas rather than on an individual's true qualifications, achievements, and merit, the recipient will never experience the true satisfaction of knowing that they earned their accomplishments. Moreover, will they ever truly earn the respect of those who earned their success? If you reward people for nothing, why expect anything?

**Nonsensical no-bids.** Some organizations offer sole-source contracts to a company rather than requiring a fair and competitive bidding process. This makes the supplier complacent and dependent over time, never having had to win the business.

**Questionable quid pro quos.** Special favors doled out through nepotism or a quid pro quo rather than earning a seat at the table have a real downside. Although the recipients of these favors may make it to the front of the line, the question remains whether they're up to the job.

**Mediocre meritocracy.** Some organizations fail to counsel mediocre performers. When people don't learn from their mistakes, their mistakes often turn into bad habits. This behavior helps neither the employees nor the organization.

**Emotional appeals.** People are often encouraged to buy from a specific source (i.e., "buy American," buy union shop, buy local), regardless of the value offered. This may kill the incentive to be more competitive, only postponing the day of reckoning when value triumphs (as it commonly does).

**Empty entitlements.** Providing government services, in some cases for generations, rather than helping people to get back on their feet and provide for themselves is a sure path to dependency and helplessness.

We are compassionate people. We should make *every* effort to help the downtrodden get back on their feet, but we shouldn't absolve them of their personal responsibility to secure a better future for themselves and their families.

Compassion shouldn't be measured by the size of a handout but by our ability to provide opportunity to reduce dependency, enabling people to become self-sufficient and helping them to realize their dreams.

When we encourage people to become *completely* dependent on the goodness of others for their livelihoods or achievements — when we reward people for lack of effort and personal initiative — we strip them of their confidence, trample on their personal dignity, and kill their will to improve themselves.  :)

"

WHILE DETERMINATION
BUILDS CHARACTER,
QUITTING IS
HABIT FORMING.

"

# DON'T QUIT. SHOW SOME GRIT

Over the course of your lifetime, you'll be faced with situations that'll test your will, challenge your determination, and define your character. Yet, even though your personal limits may be challenged, quitting shouldn't be an option. The key is to show some grit and face the situation head-on. Of course, that's easier said than done – we're all human.

The fact is, the difference between a winner and an also-ran isn't always that the loser fell on hard times – it's how the loser faced the adversity. While some people boldly stare difficulty in the eye, others are quick to surrender to it.

## ARE YOU UP TO THE TEST?

When you face a challenge, your body reacts in a very predictable manner. It's like a physical and emotional tidal wave that slams into you. Your palms get sweaty, your heart starts pounding, and an adrenaline rush kicks in. "Come on," you say to yourself, "I've seen this before." The question is, are you up to the challenge or will you quit and throw in the towel?

Don't work yourself into a frenzy. Don't let others convince you to quit. What do they know? It's amazing what you can do when you don't know you can't! Please don't underestimate the task. It won't be easy. It's important to set realistic expectations, show some grit, and follow a systematic approach from the start. You can do it. Here's how:

- First, break big challenges into bite-size pieces. They won't seem as overwhelming.

- Then, rather than setting a long-term goal, create ambitious yet achievable short-term milestones. Short-term wins will keep you motivated as you pursue your long-term goal.

- Stop procrastinating. Nothing happens until you make it happen. Don't talk about what you're going to do…do it.

- And stop focusing on whether or not you hit your goal. Instead, focus on every small win, as well as on the positive activity and energy that you're generating. Every step you take in the right direction moves you one step closer to your ultimate goal.

Close your eyes. Take a deep breath. Create a mental image of yourself achieving your goal and take the plunge. Now's the hard part. When your inner voice whispers, "It's time to give up," don't give in. When your inner voice whispers, "Just one more cigarette," or "It's only one piece of pie," whisper back, "Not this time!"

Every great performer, every athlete, every entrepreneur shares one thing in common: They achieved greatness because they had the confidence, skill, and determination to make their goal a reality. Something inside them said, "I'll never quit."

## GO FOR IT!

Reach deep down into your soul and give it all you've got. There are times when you'll reach your limit and everything inside you will tell you to stop. That's the real *moment of truth.*

Many people throw in the towel on the one-yard line, not knowing how close they were to the goal. When you get to that point, remember why you started your journey and make the extra effort to cross the goal line!

While determination builds character, quitting is habit forming. When quitting becomes routine, you won't think twice about giving up the next time. On the other hand, every time you overcome a challenge, you'll gain the strength and conviction to confront your next challenge with confidence and fortitude.

You have what it takes to be a winner. You have the courage, skill, and inner strength to face any challenge, overcome any adversity, and hang tough until the job is done. The choice is yours. If you want to be a winner, act like one. Don't quit. Show some grit. :)

> *WHAT* YOU HAVE IS MOMENTARY; *WHO* YOU ARE IS FOREVER.

# HOW WELL DO YOU REALLY KNOW YOURSELF?

As children, we love to play make-believe. We pretend to be a fireman, a doctor, or a ballerina. We fantasize about becoming a movie star, a star football player, and of course, a superhero. We love playing grown-up and imagining what we'll be when we do grow up. (Are you seeing yourself in this picture?)

As we enter early adulthood, our ambitions take on a more serious tone as we contemplate our chosen career – what we want to do and how we want to live our life. The challenge, as we see it, is to make sure our career meets our professional goals and our personal desires as well.

It's interesting to consider how much time we spend contemplating *what* we want to do and the *lifestyle* we desire and yet, how little time we spend defining *who* we want to be. The truth is, it's not *what you have*, but *who you are* that counts.

What *you have is momentary;* who *you are is forever.*

## WHO DO YOU WANT TO BE WHEN YOU GROW UP?

You may be thinking, why is that important? First, when you discover *who you want to be*, those character traits become a priority, etched on your conscience. They will influence your decisions, guide your behavior, and inspire you to achieve your full potential.

Second, if you don't identify those character traits, those signposts, you'll never know if you're on course or working against your best interest. Goals enable you to compare your progress against objectives and to adjust your behavior accordingly. As the famous cliché says, "What gets measured gets done."

Third, moral standards encourage you to remain on course. When values are top of mind, you may think twice before deviating from them – even if you can get away with it. While you may be able to fool others, you have to answer to a higher authority – your conscience. That alone may dissuade you from veering off track.

In addition, establishing yourself as a person of high moral character will boost your confidence, strengthen your relationships, and bolster your career. It will improve your health, enrich your success, and increase your happiness. Know who you are! You have to live with yourself for the rest of your life.

## THE IMPORTANCE OF KNOWING YOURSELF

Here are six valuable benefits to knowing yourself:

**Make yourself proud.** People won't respect you if you don't respect yourself. Set standards of excellence that make the most important person – you – proud.

**Achieve inner peace.** Be satisfied with what you have and who you are rather than seeking validation or living up to others' expectations. The result is that you'll spend more time listening to your inner voice than being sidetracked by others.

**Build trust.** When you know who you are, your behavior is consistent. This enables others to anticipate your behavior, which helps to build open, honest, and trusting relationships.

**Cultivate strong relationships.** Know what you stand for. Shared beliefs and values form the heart of every successful relationship and ultimately determine its success.

**Keep things in perspective.** Focus on what really matters. Possessions age and lose value over time; memories last forever.

**Live a purpose-driven life.** Follow your North Star. Identify activities that matter most to you and spend the majority of your time and effort in those areas. Cherish every moment and seek to live life without regret.

## KNOW THYSELF

One day you'll look back and reflect on your life. You'll care not only where life has taken you, but how you got there as well. You'll take great pride in knowing that you set the bar high and pursued your dreams with gusto. You'll delight in observing that you accomplished great things and did so with honor and grace. You'll relish the fact that you gave more than you took and helped to make the world a better place. At that point you'll acknowledge the fact that the real measure of success wasn't what you accumulated, but what you gave back. When you were a little kid, you fantasized that you were a superhero; now you've become one. :)

FEEDBACK TURNS GOOD INTO BETTER AND BETTER INTO BEST.

# HOW DO YOU REACT TO NEGATIVE FEEDBACK?

How do you react to being told that you did a poor job? The first option is to defend yourself and try to prove the messenger wrong. The alternative is to ask *why*? While the first option may protect your ego, the second approach demonstrates your desire to learn – and to do things better next time. How do you react to negative feedback?

If you've ever watched a dance instructor, mentor, or football coach in action, they continually offer constructive feedback to improve the recipient's game. The recipient knows full well that the feedback isn't given in malice; rather, it's an opportunity to grow. The fact is, if you don't learn from the first time you perform an activity, you'll do it the same way in the future. Practice doesn't make perfect if you're doing it wrong.

*Ask yourself, do you have 20 years of experience or one year of experience repeated 20 times?*

## 10 WAYS PEOPLE DISCOURAGE FEEDBACK

"It's uncomfortable to receive negative feedback," you might say. So you send signals that you don't want it. You rationalize that if you don't know your weaknesses, you don't have any. The reality is that closing your eyes to problems doesn't make them disappear. What you don't know *can* hurt you.

Here are 10 mindsets that can cause people to discourage feedback:

**Possessing a poor attitude.** Some people view feedback as a slap in the face.

**Acting self-important.** Some folks think they know it all.

**Being worried about one's reputation.** Some people feel that requesting feedback is a sign of weakness and will reflect poorly on them.

**Being introverted.** Some folks are too timid or shy to ask for feedback.

**Acting delusional.** Some people think that if they don't know their faults, they don't have any.

**Displaying arrogance.** Some folks think they're superior. "What do others know, anyway?"

**Being self-critical.** Some people believe that having flaws constitutes failure.

**Feeling too busy.** Some folks don't have time for feedback – even if it makes them more effective.

**Displaying a lack of self-confidence.** Some people don't want to be *judged* – even if it's constructive.

**Being lazy.** Some folks believe that if they don't *ask* for feedback, they don't have to *act* on it.

## TREAT FEEDBACK AS A GIFT RATHER THAN AS A SLAP IN THE FACE

When you think you're superior, when you're too timid or shy, when you act like a know-it-all, and when you don't have time to request feedback, the result is the same. You become blind to your flaws, and your weaknesses become permanent.

> *When people don't learn from mistakes,
> their mistakes often turn into bad habits.*

You can get feedback from a role model, mentor, friend, family member, teacher, coach, customer, supervisor – the list goes on. The simple way to look at feedback is if you had the opportunity to do an activity again, how could you perform it better?

It's important to note that negative feedback is the first step toward personal growth. The only thing worse than not *requesting* feedback is not *acting* on it. When you ask for feedback, and fail to act on it, you discourage people from offering it to you again in the future. That doesn't mean you have to implement everything suggested. But when folks give of their time to help you, the least you should do is circle back with them.

## LEARNING IS AS MUCH AN ATTITUDE AS IT IS AN ACTIVITY

It doesn't matter whether you're an experienced old-timer, top executive, rising star, or master teacher, you always have something to learn. Most people who make it to the top of their game do so, in part, by viewing feedback as an opportunity to better themselves – rather than as criticism or a cause for embarrassment. They know that lessons in life will be repeated until they are learned.

Here's some free advice. If you discourage negative feedback, you're only hurting yourself. In effect, you're saying that you've made it to the top of your game so there's no room for improvement. Once you say that, one thing is clear: You've seen your finest hour and are on your way down. The converse is also true. Feedback turns good into better and better into best.  :)

"

PULL OUT THE WEEDS,
OR MAKE PEACE
WITH THE
DANDELIONS.

# 30 HABITS THAT CREATE ENORMOUS DISTRESS

Most things in life are the result of choices that we make. In other words, life doesn't happen *to* you; it's created *by* you. Here are 30 habits that create enormous distress. Do any of these sound familiar?

Do you:

**Live beyond your means?** When you run out of money, stop buying.

**Fail to honor commitments?** Keep those promises that you make to others – and to yourself.

**Worry about tomorrow?** If you can't change the outcome, move on to an area within your control.

**Dodge personal responsibility?** If you look in the mirror and don't like what you see, don't blame the mirror. It's your life to live. Own it!

**Take things for granted?** Be happy with what you *have* rather than obsessing about what you *don't* have.

**Fear leaving your comfort zone?** The old adage rings true: It's not the things you *do* in life that you regret, it's the things you *don't* do.

**Fail to act?** Dreams, unlike eggs, don't hatch from sitting on them.

**Crave approval and validation from others?** When you constantly seek approval, you give more weight to another person's opinion than to your own.

**Betray your beliefs and values?** Know what matters most to you and be unwilling to compromise those priorities at any price.

**Compare yourself to others?** Don't compare yourself to others. It only breeds envy and resentment. When you compete with yourself, you both win.

**Feel guilty saying "no"?** The more you say "no" to things that don't matter, the more time you have for things that do.

**Value possessions over relationships?** Moments, rather than possessions, are the true treasures of life.

**Criticize yourself?** Don't be too tough on yourself. Why would you say something to yourself that you wouldn't say to a good friend?

**Harbor anger?** Set yourself free. Forgiving doesn't mean forgetting, or approving of, what someone did. It just means that you're letting go of the anger toward that person.

**Think you know everything?** When you think you've learned it all, you'll discover how much you really don't know.

**Act like a slave to your money?** Money should never become the cornerstone of your life or define you as a person. It's a means to support yourself and your family.

**Feel entitled?** People who receive a free lunch end up paying the price. If you're rewarded *without effort*, it reduces confidence, promotes dependency, and robs you of your personal dignity.

**Set the bar low?** It doesn't cost more to strive for excellence, but if you settle for mediocrity, it'll cost you dearly.

**Keep bad company?** Just as toxic waste impacts the environment, toxic people can impact your life.

**Need instant gratification?** Don't forgo your long-term dreams to satisfy your short-term desires.

**Let success go to your head?** Your ego should never equal more than one-half of your accomplishments.

**Take, take, take?** Greed can be the unwillingness to give OR the willingness to take.

**Fail to set priorities?** Determine what's important to you or you'll *react* to situations rather than make conscious decisions based on sound reasoning.

**Live on the edge?** Those living on the edge never fear falling off. When you bet against the statistics, you'll eventually become one.

**Fail to learn from mistakes?** Lessons in life will be repeated until they're learned.

**Fear failure?** Mistakes don't make you a failure, but beating yourself up makes you feel like one.

**Live to work?** Make a life while making a living.

**Act like a show-off?** The more you try to impress someone, the less impressive you become.

**Follow others' agendas?** When you spend more time doing have-to's rather than want-to's, other people's happiness becomes more important than your own.

**Compromise your integrity?** Everything has a price, but *not* everything should be for sale. Listen to your conscience. That's why you have one.

If some of these items sound familiar, determine what you'll do about it. The choice is yours: Pull out the weeds, or make peace with the dandelions. :)

"

YOUR EGO SHOULD NEVER EQUAL MORE THAN ONE-HALF OF YOUR ACCOMPLISHMENTS.

"

# THE COSTS OF A BIG EGO

Being successful is great. But having a big ego can be a detriment to that success. Here are 13 costs of a big ego:

**Weak relationships.** People with big egos can be condescending, rude, and disrespectful. Their nastiness can suck the oxygen out of a room.

**Shallow connections.** It's hard to build deep, trusting relationships when people dominate conversations, spend little time listening, and are totally self-absorbed. You gain more by making others look good than by singing your own praises.

**Inadequate knowledge.** People who think they know it all are more likely to stagnate because they undervalue the importance of acquiring knowledge.

**Blind to weaknesses.** When you swallow your pride, don't choke on your ego. People who reject feedback are more likely to repeat mistakes because they're totally blind to their flaws. In fact, ego can obstruct a necessary course correction and lead to failure.

**Ineffective decision making.** People with huge egos rarely seek advice from others – because *they* know better. They're more inclined to make decisions from a limited perspective.

**Dangerous complacency.** People with egos think they'll always remain on top. They rarely glance over their shoulder to see if competitors are gaining ground.

**Poor image.** People who blow their own horn, talk down to people, and make fun of the less fortunate will very quickly develop a poor reputation.

**Mediocre career advancement.** People with big egos are unwilling to start at the bottom; they turn down work that's "beneath them"; and they refuse to be told what to do. Then they wonder why they're passed over for promotions.

**Wrong partners.** When people have an inflated view of themselves or their organization, they're more inclined to squeeze partners than to create win-win relationships.

**Loneliness.** People who think they're above it all consciously separate themselves from others. This can lead to a lonely existence.

**Ineffective leadership.** How you handle success says a lot about you. Effective leaders build and exude confidence while keeping their ego in check. When leaders squash input, hoard the credit, and put people down, it can – and usually does – dampen the effectiveness of a team.

**Increased stress.** Some people feel they have something to prove and always have to be right. It's a coping mechanism to deal with their insecurity. The insatiable need to prove themselves is exhausting!

**Distorted self-image.** People with large egos measure self-worth based on what they've gained rather than what they've given back. That can distort their values and skew their priorities. Your ego should never equal more than one-half of your accomplishments. :)

ACHIEVING SUCCESS
DOESN'T SAY AS
MUCH ABOUT YOU
AS HOW YOU
CHOOSE TO WEAR IT.

# IS YOUR CONFIDENCE TURNING INTO EGOTISM?

Do you know any people who have a big ego? They constantly blow their own horn, fight to be the center of attention, and believe they're always right, even when they're not. They think they know it all, steer every conversation their way, and believe that the world revolves around them. Right? In fact, they have such an inflated view of themselves that they can't wait to tell you how wonderful they are and how successful they've become. They may have everything in the world going for them, but the egotism is tough to take. (Ugh!)

Many people buy into the common misconception that confidence and egotism are the same thing. The truth is, confident people believe in themselves and their abilities, while egocentric folks have inflated opinions of themselves and care only about their personal interests.

Being successful is great, but having a big ego can be a detriment to that success. It can tarnish your relationships, restrict your personal growth, weaken your leadership performance, damage your career advancement, and the list goes on.

*The more you try to impress someone, the less impressive you become.*

## KEEP YOUR EGO IN CHECK

Having confidence is important, but it's critical that you keep your confidence from turning into egotism. Here are 16 ways to keep your ego in check:

**Challenge yourself.** Strive to be the best you can be...and then be a little better.

**Surround yourself with talented people.** Surround yourself with exceptional people. Don't view them as a threat. Let them challenge you to be your best.

**Give up control.** Have faith in your colleagues. You can't do everything yourself.

**Make yourself vulnerable.** Send signals that you don't know it all. Achieve this by asking for help and soliciting input from others.

**Identify weaknesses.** Solicit feedback to help address your personal deficiencies and mistakes. But remember to act on that input!

**Share credit.** Acknowledge others to demonstrate that it takes more than one person to achieve success.

**Get real!** Accept praise and the good feeling that it brings, while remembering that you are no better than anyone else.

**Keep yourself on your toes.** Don't let your guard down and become complacent. It's easier to maintain momentum than to rebuild it once it's lost.

**Earn respect.** You can't *demand* respect; you earn it.

**Remember your roots.** Think of all the people who contributed to your success. As you climb your ladder, reach down and pull others along with you.

**Be discreet.** If you do something nice, do it quietly. You defeat the purpose when you boast about your generosity.

**Listen to your friends.** Real friends will always give it to you straight. Your job is to listen up!

**Reflect on your behavior.** Rein in your ego by listening to your conscience.

**Be modest.** If you're really good, people know. There's no need to blow your own horn. Your ego should never be more than one-half of your accomplishments.

**Laugh at yourself.** See the humor in everything. Don't take yourself so seriously.

**Recognize the impermanence of everything.** Nothing lasts forever. As Vince Gill, the American country singer, said, "Success is always temporary. When all is said and done, the only thing you'll have left is your character."

## CHECK YOUR EGO AT THE DOOR

The purpose of this essay is NOT to denigrate success. If your success was earned through hard work and honesty, never apologize for it. BUT, achieving success doesn't say as much about you as how you choose to wear it.

> *Those who serve arrogance as their main course*
> *will eat humble pie for dessert.*

When you reach your goals, there's no need to brag about your achievements or rub your success in the face of others. Instead, take a moment to smile inside so that you're the only one who can see it. You don't have to win the applause of others because you've already attained so much more – self-respect and inner peace. Bravo! You can hold your head up high knowing that your hard work and commitment paid off. There's no need to boast about your achievements because acting with humility and grace says volumes about you. :)

"

THERE ARE TWO SIDES TO EVERY STORY — ESPECIALLY IF YOU'RE A HYPOCRITE.

"

# ARE YOU A HYPOCRITE?

Do you know any people who are as phony as a three-dollar bill? They say one thing yet do another; they make rules but don't follow them; and they live one way in public yet another in private. They're so dishonest, they could be called professional liars. In fact, many hypocrites even lie to themselves.

Sometimes folks are unaware that they're being two-faced, but oftentimes they know exactly what they're doing. They're trying to manipulate the truth, conceal an embarrassment, or compensate for a weak line of reasoning. In any case, hypocrites know the real truth, but they're afraid that revealing it may have negative consequences – so they mislead.

*There are two sides to every story – especially if you're a hypocrite.*

## 23 WAYS TO SPOT A HYPOCRITE

Hypocrites quickly give themselves away by their behavior. Here are 23 ways to spot one.

Hypocrites:

- Say one thing but do another.

- Treat those in power differently than they treat underlings.
- Give advice but fail to follow their own guidance.
- Preach tolerance but judge others who don't conform to their way of thinking.
- Volunteer others but *rarely* raise their own hand.
- Live one way in public but another in private.
- Pretend to be someone they're not *merely* to win acceptance.
- Make rules but fail to follow the rules themselves.
- Preach morality but live a shameful life.
- Demand things of others that they're unwilling to do themselves.
- Say one thing to someone's face but another thing behind their back.
- Pretend to be wealthy even though their bank account is scanty.
- Alter their opinion to gain acceptance from people with differing viewpoints.
- Condemn the actions of others even though they commit those same acts themselves.
- Promote a holier-than-thou image *merely* to offset reckless behavior.
- Help people *only* when it's in their personal interest to do so.
- Pretend to care even when their motive is really self-serving.
- Demand austerity for others but handsomely compensate themselves.
- Feign outrage even though they have no intention of doing anything about it.

- Penalize some folks for wrongdoing but look the other way for everyone else.
- Lecture people about morality but cover up for their friends.
- Judge others but call people intolerant when they're personally judged.
- Act one way when folks are looking, the opposite when they're not.

## BE TRUE TO YOURSELF AND TO OTHERS

Hypocrisy is an addiction. You dupe people once and think you can get away with it again. But although you may think that you're fooling the world, you're only kidding yourself. People are on to you, and the ramifications are worse than you think.

How can you be a trusted friend, respected parent, credible role model, or an effective leader if you're living a lie? As the saying goes, "Some people are like pennies. Two-faced and worthless."

Authentic people are genuine – they're confident in their beliefs and are true to themselves. People who have strength of conviction don't obstruct the truth. They don't fear what people may think, what folks may say, or that some people may challenge or reject their views. They are true to their principles, own their actions, and most importantly, they're true to themselves. Period!

Be the real you. Listen to your conscience. Form your own opinions. And live your life with honor. One of the best rewards from achieving success is knowing that you earned your achievements through hard work, commitment, and integrity. The same is true of living a good life. Believe in yourself. Be authentic. Live the truth! At the end of the day, be proud of what you do and who you are. After all, you have to live with yourself for the rest of your life. :)

"

YOU'D BE PERFECT
IF YOU WEREN'T
A PERFECTIONIST.

"

# WHEN YOU'RE A PERFECTIONIST, YOUR WORK IS NEVER DONE

Is being called a *perfectionist* all it's cracked up to be? If you're a perfectionist, it means that you strive for perfection in everything you do. It's never good enough to do your best; the outcome must be perfect – nothing less. It doesn't matter whether you're working on a simple project, raising your children, or searching for an answer, the end result can't be just "good"; it must be flawless…impeccable… picture perfect. Period.

And there's the rub. If you're a perfectionist, you believe the *ultimate standard must* be achieved every time you do anything. It doesn't matter whether your goal is large or small, essential or trivial, urgent or routine, you'll go to the ends of the earth to surpass excellence. Is it worth it?

*When you're a perfectionist, your work is never done.*

## ARE YOU A PERFECTIONIST?

Question yourself on the following…think about how you:

**Perform an activity.** Are you uncomfortable saying, "I'm finished" – because an activity can always be improved?

**Manage relationships.** Do you judge people on a regular basis and find fault in most of them?

**Make an everyday purchase.** Do you search forever when making a *minor* purchase? Do you read every product review and spend hours looking for the cheapest price?

**Raise your kids.** Do you compare your kids to others and then push your kids beyond their limits?

**Seek advice.** Do you ask everyone for advice just to ensure that you don't miss anything?

**Manage a project.** Do you delegate responsibility and then micromanage people because you just can't let go?

**Rate your performance.** Do you hold yourself to an impossible standard and beat yourself up for minor mistakes?

## YOU'D BE PERFECT IF YOU WEREN'T A PERFECTIONIST

Here are 10 reasons why being a perfectionist is far from perfect:

**Low productivity.** If you begin things, but never complete them, you accomplish nothing.

**Get down on yourself.** If you create *unrealistic* expectations for yourself, you're likely to damage your confidence and self-image. In addition, no matter what you achieve, the feeling of satisfaction will be temporary because you'll raise the bar again.

**Loss of opportunity.** If you adopt an attitude of "If I *can't* do it perfectly, then I won't even try," you'll let opportunities pass you by. In addition, if you take too much time achieving perfection, you'll miss out to a faster competitor.

**Hard to make decisions.** If you overwhelm yourself with information, you may become indecisive.

**Afraid to delegate.** If you think you're the only one who can do things right, you'll probably end up doing everything yourself.

**Invest more time than required.** If you try to achieve perfection by performing *needless tasks*, you'll add needless stress and drive yourself crazy.

**Create a money-losing proposition.** If you spend unreasonable time and effort making things perfect, it may be impossible to recoup those costs from customers.

**Demoralize others.** If you're highly critical of others, you'll discourage them from spending time with you.

**Short-sightedness.** If you spend too much time meticulously reviewing details, you'll end up missing the big picture.

**Waste of time.** If you spend an inordinate amount of time on stupid stuff, you won't have time to devote to things that matter.

## STRIVE FOR EXCELLENCE, NOT PERFECTION

If you're a perfectionist, you probably make everything into a competition – always pushing – never satisfied. Take a moment to consider whether that mindset is a net positive or a net negative in your life. What are the incremental benefits of choosing perfection over excellence? What do you lose in the process? Think about the toll that it's taking on your life and whether the return is worth it to you.

Hold yourself up to a high standard, not an impossible one. If you believe the only way to obtain inner peace and tranquility is by making everything perfect on the outside, you may be sadly mistaken. When you constantly have to prove your worth – even to yourself – you're creating an impossible scenario in which the finish line is constantly moving. In conclusion, if you believe that excellence isn't good enough, you may wake up one day and realize that your quest for perfection was anything but perfect. :)

"

# ONE OF THE GREATEST REWARDS OF SUCCESS IS KNOWING THAT THE HARD-FOUGHT VICTORY WAS EARNED.

"

## YOU DESERVE IT, BUT...

You hit the ground running, worked your butt off, and did everything required of you. And in the end, you exceeded expectations and hit the ball out of the park. It's only natural that you expect to be recognized and rewarded for your efforts. After all, you deserve it! But what if you're not? What if that reward is given to someone else – someone with inferior results? How would that make you feel?

The truth is, when rewards are granted based on popularity, bias, or cronyism, rather than on tangible results, it sends a message loud and clear – you got screwed!

> *People stop trying when there's no benefit for being exceptional and no consequence for being mediocre.*

### 10 WAYS WINNERS LOSE

It's no different than a gymnastic championship. Imagine if you practiced tirelessly, competed fiercely, and outperformed your competitor, yet were sent home a loser. (Just because you won the championship the prior two years, the judges decided to give the win to your rival.) Is that fair?

Here are 10 ways you could lose – even though you won:

**Favoritism.** Favoritism gives unfair preferential treatment to a person or group at the expense of another. It's not *what* you know. It's *who* you know.

**Social status.** Social rank is based on someone's position in society rather than on their character, ability, or achievements.

**Popularity.** Preferential treatment is given to those who are liked, admired, or supported by the masses.

**Cronyism.** Friends and associates are granted favors, without regard to qualifications or merit.

**Tenure.** Special treatment is awarded based on years of employment rather than on performance or achievement.

**Nepotism.** Relatives or friends receive preferential treatment.

**Coercion.** Whoever shouts the loudest forces a hearing – or in this case, a reward.

**Fixed quotas.** Outcome is based on a predetermined number or percentage rather than on qualifications or merit. It's hard to demand equality and expect special treatment.

**Bias.** Prejudice is shown in favor of or against a person or group compared to another.

**Pay to play.** People buy their way to the table. They receive special favors because they're willing to pay for them.

## FREE CAN BE COSTLY

Let's look at it from the flip side: How can you command the trust, admiration, and respect of others when you receive special treatment? How can you do your job properly when everyone knows that your rewards were unearned? How can you face yourself in the mirror knowing full well that you're living a lie? Rewards are meaningless if they're not deserved.

*When undeserving people win,
the real loser is the so-called winner.*

If you receive a handout or have a silver spoon in your mouth, you're disincentivized from working hard. Why bother paying your dues if rewards are served to you on a silver platter? The truth is, freebies create complacency and a false sense of security. What looks like a gift is merely a Trojan horse. Before you can say "free lunch," your knowledge goes stale, your skills weaken, and your passion wanes. Essentially, you are robbed of your personal dignity and self-worth. Meanwhile, the message being sent to others is loud and clear as well. Why make the effort if it's not appreciated? After all, people are getting rewarded based on favoritism, cronyism, and popularity.

*Winning without honor is worse than a loss.*

## DO YOU REWARD FOLKS WHO DESERVE IT?

If you really want to be helpful and compassionate, don't tip the balance in someone's favor. Instead, give them the tools and self-confidence they need to succeed in the real world. Simply put, promote the importance of moral character, give them a first-class education and training, inspire them to achieve great things, hold them to the same *high* standard as others, and get out of the way. In essence, make them earn their success! It'll promote self-reliance; it'll do wonders for their self-image; and it'll enhance their ability to function in the real world. One of the greatest rewards of success is knowing that the hard-fought victory was earned. They deserve that! :)

"

LOOK IN THE MIRROR
RATHER THAN AT
YOUR NEIGHBOR.

"

# DO YOU LET ENVY GET THE BETTER OF YOU?

If you could trade places with anyone, who would it be? Why would you select that individual over others? Is it because of their personality, relationships, possessions, career achievements, or their overall lifestyle? The million-dollar question is: Do you *admire* that person or do you envy that person?

In the age of social media, it's hard to ignore what your neighbor is doing. After all, most folks reveal their entire life on social media. To make it worse, some people can't keep their ego in check. For example, people brag about their expensive possessions, lavish experiences, luxurious vacations, perfect relationships, and of course, their physical attractiveness. (Yuck!) Everyone knows that some of their blabber is exaggerated, but it's not unusual to think others have it better than you. That can take a toll on your confidence.

Your self-image and self-worth are influenced, in part, by comparing yourself to others. It's also determined by contrasting *who you are* against *who you want to be*. That comparison can go one of two ways. It can be *beneficial* – inspiring you to become a better person. Or it can be *detrimental* – making you envious and resentful of others.

"They have more,
 They have it easier,
 They have it better,
 They have it all," you may think.

*Resentment can make you bitter rather than
encouraging you to be your best.*

## ENVY IS TOXIC AND DESTRUCTIVE

It's hard to admit that someone could be more deserving of a good life than you. To rationalize that sentiment, some folks denounce *successful people* – saying they didn't really earn their accomplishments. They "received an unfair advantage" or "secured their achievements by mistreating others."

If you subscribe to that notion, you may conclude that *life is unfair* and that others are holding you back; this frees you from having to accept personal responsibility for your circumstances. Such thinking can lead to envy, resentment, and even anger.

While you may think that envious behavior is warranted, harboring resentment can hurt you more than you think. For example, it can:

**Distort your sense of reality.** If you believe you're being treated unfairly, you'll look for proof that supports your view. That thinking can progress into a downward spiral, making you angrier and more envious rather than positive and constructive. Furthermore, if you surround yourself with like-minded people, they'll reinforce those beliefs, making it harder for you to shed that unproductive mindset.

**Hurt your health.** If you're gloomy about your future, you'll view every opportunity as a glass half-empty rather than as a glass half-full. That can be debilitating and have a negative impact on your psyche.

According to the Mayo Clinic, positive thinking can increase your life span, lower rates of depression, offer better psychological and physical well-being, reduce the risk of death from cardiovascular disease, and enable you to cope better during hardships and times of stress.*

**Destroy positive relationships.** Envy can turn friends into adversaries. If you think your friends' accomplishments were achieved unfairly, you'll resent them for their triumphs rather than be happy for their success.

**Foster unproductive behavior.** If you become consumed with envy, you may be motivated to seek retribution, and tear others down, even though *their* success may have no correlation to *your* success.

**Damage your opportunity for success and happiness.** If you believe the world is against you, you'll be more inclined to give up than to invest in your future.

## LOOK IN THE MIRROR RATHER THAN AT YOUR NEIGHBOR

Just as you'll never really understand someone's problems until you walk a mile in their shoes, you'll never fully appreciate the effort and commitment that someone made to achieve their success. Moreover, the *more* time you spend comparing yourself to others, the *less* time you'll have to make your own dreams come true.

> *If the grass is greener on the other side of the fence, chances are it's getting better care.*

There will always be people who have more, or less, than you. Get over it. Be grateful for what you have. Money should never become the cornerstone of your life nor should it define you as a person. It's not what you *have*, but who you *are* that counts. The only way that you'll achieve happiness is when you're at peace with yourself and thankful for the blessings in your life. :)

---

*https://www.mayoclinic.org/healthy-lifestyle/stress-management/in-depth/positive-thinking/art-20043950

> WHILE YOU MAY THINK IMPATIENT BEHAVIOR IS MOVING YOU FORWARD, IT MAY ACTUALLY BE HOLDING YOU BACK.

# ARE YOU RUNNING OUT OF PATIENCE?

It seems like yesterday that written communication was sent by mail; food was reheated on a stove; and you traveled all the way to a store to buy merchandise. Now, if you're like most people, you get frustrated when email takes a moment to appear in your inbox, the microwave takes a few seconds to beep, or a website requires a second click to complete your online purchase. Patience, what's that?

With time at a premium, it seems like patience is out with the horse and buggy. For example, people change car lanes to save a minute, eat energy bars to avoid preparing meals, and switch websites because it takes an additional second to load. Sound familiar?

## THINGS TAKE TIME TO HATCH

If a recipe says something should be cooked for 34 minutes, you can't take it out of the oven in 25. The same remains true in other areas of your life. Things require patience. Here are 15 situations in which patience is ill-treated:

**Deadlines.** Some people scream "URGENT" even when it's not required. Then, when an emergency actually arises, their plea for help falls on deaf ears. Do you cry wolf?

**Trust.** Some folks *force* a relationship rather than taking the time to establish trust. Consistent and predictable behavior breeds trust. That requires time.

**Solutions.** Some people seek a quick-fix solution rather than addressing a problem's root cause. While it may feel comforting to "do something," it's fruitless if the underlying issue isn't addressed.

**Brainstorming.** Some folks stop brainstorming when someone provides the first satisfactory response. The problem is, you'll never know if you arrived at the best answer if you cut the process short.

**Risk.** Some people swing for the fence rather than opt for the slow and steady path to success. They focus so much on striking it rich that they ignore the possible consequences of going for broke.

**Self-reliance.** Some folks create dependency rather than making people self-sufficient. As the proverb says, "Give a man a fish and he will eat for a day. Teach a man how to fish and you feed him for a lifetime."

**Business relationships.** Some people try to gain the upper hand rather than forging win-win relationships. Partnerships succeed when both parties work for the common good rather than trying to outmaneuver each other.

**Management.** Some managers *order* employees around rather than securing buy-in and commitment. Superior results are achieved when people are involved and committed.

**Speed.** Some folks sacrifice quality for speed. Crossing things off your list may be satisfying, but redoing activities takes time, too. Do it right the first time.

**Communication.** Some people talk before thinking. Doug Larson, columnist and editor, said, "Wisdom is the reward you get for a lifetime of listening when you'd have preferred to talk."

**Problem solving.** Some folks would rather throw money at a problem than come up with an effective solution.

**Success.** Some people cut corners rather than prospering through hard work, commitment, and sacrifice. The fact is, there are simply no shortcuts in the long run.

**Career.** Some folks are so impatient, they're unwilling to start at the bottom. If you want to climb the corporate ladder, you must pay your dues.

**Planning.** Some people can't be bothered with planning. They want action! Their motto is "Ready, fire, aim."

**Conscience.** Some folks are like bulldozers – they'll do anything to get ahead. Follow your conscience. You have to live with yourself for the rest of your life.

## THE POWER OF PATIENCE

In most cases, people are impatient because they think it's in their best interest and will get them to their goal faster. The truth is quite to the contrary. While you may think impatient behavior is moving you forward, it may actually be holding you back.

*Patience is like a muscle – the more you exercise it,*
*the greater it becomes.*

Be patient. Take a moment to think. Gain some perspective. Plan before you proceed. And only then, move forward with resolve. You'll find these steps work wonders for you. Patience will enhance your relationships, increase your productivity, and improve your mental health. I know it's not easy. But some of the hardest things in life are also the most worthwhile. As Saadi Shirazi, a Persian poet, said, "Have patience. All things are difficult before they become easy." :)

"

**WORDS EXPRESS WHAT'S ON YOUR MIND, BUT YOUR ACTIONS SAY WHAT'S IN YOUR HEART.**

"

## HOW TO MAKE YOUR WORDS MEANINGFUL

Your words express your thoughts, your feelings, and your dreams. Those words come in many forms – long or short, plentiful or few – and they can be heartfelt or phony. Once in a while, a simple look, a glancing nod, or even a hug says more than your words can express. What's more, there are times when no words can express your happiness or voice your sorrow.

*Silence can say everything.*

Once words leave your mouth, they're seldom forgotten. As the saying goes, "You can't unring a bell." So be careful what you say or you may live to regret it one day. What's more, words on paper take on a life of their own. They can last a lifetime…and even longer.

One thing is certain *in every language*: You can say things till you're blue in the face, BUT your words are meaningless if they *conflict* with your actions.

*Words express what's on your mind,*
*but your actions say what's in your heart.*

## A WORD TO THE WISE

People spout out about niceties such as showing gratitude, building trust, or being tolerant. But those words are meaningless if they're not part of your daily ritual. Do you preach about morality, but fail to live up to the standards that you set for others? Do you make commitments, but fail to keep them as promised? Do you lecture people about civility and tolerance, but bite off the head of someone who disagrees with you? Do you often condemn folks for being self-centered and greedy, but fail to raise your own hand to volunteer? In other words, do you live by your words or just talk a good game?

*Some folks who prescribe tolerance should take their own medicine.*

While your words may say volumes about you, your actions say even more. The true meaning of your words is *not* what you say, but what you do. Your words are most meaningful when they mirror your actions…and vice versa. Take my word for it. :)

" YOU CAN SAY THINGS TILL YOU'RE BLUE IN THE FACE, BUT YOUR WORDS ARE MEANINGLESS IF THEY CONFLICT WITH YOUR ACTIONS. "

> **THINK ABOUT THE BEST WAY TO COMMUNICATE YOUR MESSAGE BEFOREHAND OR GET READY TO DO SOME DAMAGE CONTROL AFTERWARD.**

# HERE'S AN IMPORTANT MESSAGE FOR YOU

Would you use voicemail to fire someone, recite your marriage vows in an email, or end a romantic relationship via text? Of course not. But unfortunately, these communication media are used inappropriately every day. The fact is, each form of communication has its advantages and disadvantages. When it comes to communication, one size *doesn't* fit all.

*The best tools are useless if they're not used properly.*

## WHAT ARE YOU TRYING TO ACHIEVE?

Before you select the right communication medium, there are many factors to consider: Is the subject matter important or trivial? Is the communication urgent? Is the issue sensitive? Will one person or several people be involved? What's the availability of your contact(s)? Will the communication be primarily one way (a directive) or is dialogue necessary? Is there a need to keep a written record of the exchange?

**Face-to-face conversation.** There's nothing like a face-to-face conversation for building a relationship, discussing sensitive information, or making sure that everyone's on the same page.

Face-to-face conversations enable you to look into someone's eyes while they're talking, hear the inflection in their voice, and observe their body language. But meeting individually with several people may be costly and logistically difficult to engineer.

**Telephone calls and video chats.** If you're catching up with busy people in various locations, telephone calls and video chats are very efficient modes of communication. Plus, when the subject matter is important, or sensitive items are discussed, these modes facilitate two-way dialogue. The fact is, being able to hear voice inflection and sense the sender's intent helps to avoid misunderstandings that can occur with written communication. A video chat takes it one step further and enables you to pick up on nonverbal cues. But I can assure you that no one's sitting around waiting for your call. So advance notice is important, or the individual might not be available to take your call – think phone tag.

**Social media.** Remember how easy it was to keep in touch with friends when you were in college? Of course, when everyone went their separate ways, it became harder to remain in touch; that is, until social media hit the scene. Now, you can make new friends and stay in touch with old ones – right from your living room.

Social media makes it easy to exchange small talk, share an article or video, or join a discussion group. And you can be an active participant or a fly on the wall. But remember, if you are having a sensitive conversation or ranting about an issue close to your heart, beware. Your five hundred closest friends may be listening in. Furthermore, many people think that once a post is deleted, it's gone forever. Unfortunately, that's not true. Your digital footprint may catch up with you one day.

**Email.** When you write an email, you can ensure that your message is "perfectly" worded before hitting "Send." And the recipient can read it at their convenience — alleviating phone tag. In addition, email provides a record of the conversation if you think you might need to refer back to it one day. But emails can create misunderstandings because you can't hear the tone of the sender's voice or see their body language.

**Texting.** If you have an urgent request, want to remind someone to bring home milk, or let someone know that you arrived at your destination safely, texting is great. Remember: If you can say it in a paragraph, don't write a book. But it's less than optimal if you're conducting a serious conversation or explaining something in detail. Plus, although it may be a convenient time for you to send the text, unlike email, when it flashes on your screen you may be interrupting the recipient during a busy time.

The bottom line: According to UCLA research, 55 percent of meaning in an interaction comes from facial and body language and 38 percent comes from vocal inflection. Only 7 percent of an interaction's meaning is derived from the words themselves.*

## BETTER COMMUNICATION: A WAKE-UP CALL

Please don't get wedded to one form of communication because you're familiar with it. The next time you have something to say, you have a choice: Think about the best way to communicate your message beforehand or get ready to do some damage control afterward. :)

---

*https://en.wikipedia.org/wiki/Albert_Mehrabian

"
WHEN YOU TAKE THINGS FOR GRANTED, YOU DIMINISH THEIR IMPORTANCE AND MAY EVEN JEOPARDIZE THEIR VERY EXISTENCE.
"

# ARE YOU GRATEFUL?

Some people are grateful for their possessions, such as a car, a fine wardrobe, or the phone that seems like it's another appendage of their body. Others are thankful for being able to live in a nice neighborhood, take lovely vacations, or enjoy the many rewards of their new promotion. But the truth is, *too many of us take other, very important, things for granted* – simply because we've enjoyed their benefits for so long. If these things disappeared, however, it would leave a significant void in our lives.

## BE GRATEFUL

**Bare necessities.** Some people don't experience the luxury of having food, shelter, heat, electricity, or running water. You may view these things as nothing special, but those without them sure don't.

**True love.** Some folks go all out during the early phase of a relationship, only to neglect it over time. That's their loss.

**Personal responsibility.** Some people view personal responsibility as a burden and outsource their freedom to others. You are the master of your destiny; they're not.

**Quality time.** Some folks are happiest being on the run. If you don't take the time to cherish precious moments, your whole life will be a blur.

**Peace of mind.** Some folks will do *anything* and step on *anyone* to get what they want. The one thing ruthless people rarely get is a good night's sleep.

**Steady income.** Some people complain about work like complaining is their job. Although they don't seem to appreciate a steady paycheck, think about the alternative.

**Free time.** Some folks are bored when they have nothing to do. Life is not a race to the finish line. Happiness is a result of balance rather than intensity.

**Fond memories.** Some people would trade anything for money. Moments, rather than possessions, are the true treasures of life.

**Family time.** Some people have no time for their kids. Then they're surprised when their kids don't have time for them.

**Caring friends.** Some folks take their friendships for granted. If they continue along this path, they'll be spending a lot of time alone.

**Good health.** Some folks take their good health for granted. Take care of your body. It's the only one you've got.

**Money in the bank.** Some people fail to appreciate the value of savings. Then, when a little rain shower appears, it feels like a storm.

**Clear conscience.** Some folks take inner peace for granted. Follow your conscience. Sleep well.

**Life.** Some people worry so much about tomorrow that they forget to love life today. Life is like playing musical chairs – you never know when the music will stop.

**Freedom.** If you were born in a different place or at a different time, you might not enjoy the right to speak freely, to practice your religion, to bear arms, to enjoy a free press, or to be viewed as *equal* with others in the eyes of the law. In addition, you might not be able to own property, dress how you please, marry whomever you want, or vote for the candidate of your choice. Furthermore, you might not be free to make your own choices, be who you want to be, access information, or travel wherever and whenever you'd like. The list is endless. I wish your gratitude would be, too.

## BE GRATEFUL AND COUNT YOUR BLESSINGS

One of the reasons why people fail to appreciate their personal situation is that they're too busy comparing themselves to others. The fact is, there will always be people with more or less than you have. That should never be the measure of happiness. When you take things for granted, you diminish their importance and may even jeopardize their very existence.

*Is your satisfaction based on what you* have
*or are you obsessed with what you* don't *have?*

Do you ever take the time to think about how lucky you are? Take a moment and recognize all the wonderful things in your life. They don't have to have large monetary value. In fact, some of the little things are those that matter the most. As Frank A. Clark, the politician, said, "If a fellow isn't thankful for what he's got, he isn't likely to be thankful for what he's going to get."  :)

> THE ONLY DIFFERENCE BETWEEN BEING UNINFORMED AND BEING MISINFORMED IS THAT ONE IS *YOUR* CHOICE AND THE OTHER IS *THEIRS*.

# DO YOU LIVE IN THE DARK?

Close your eyes. What do you see? Nothing? Let me ask you a different way: Close your office door. What's happening outside your four walls? You're not sure, you say? The fact is, when you live behind closed doors; when you build walls around yourself; when you're close-minded and tune out others' viewpoints; and when you act like a know-it-all, ignoring input and feedback, the result is the same. You're living in the dark.

If you think tuning others out is positive, in any way, you're sadly mistaken. When you avoid feedback, shut down debate, or fail to request input, it's counterproductive.

*What you don't know* can *hurt you.*

## DO YOU KNOW YOUR BLIND SPOTS?

Are you stifling your ability to learn and make progress? How many of these 10 barriers sound familiar?

Do you resist feedback?
Are you too busy to listen?
Are you a know-it-all?
Do you seek input from limited sources?

Do you shut people out to protect your feelings?
Do you get defensive when people offer feedback?
Do you seek input *only* from people with status?
Do you let your ego stop you from requesting input?
Do you surround yourself with "yes" people?
Do you think negative feedback is another way of saying, "You failed"?

## OPEN YOUR EYES AND OPEN YOUR MIND

If you're living in the dark, it's time to get a reality check. Here are 10 tips to enlighten you:

**Get personal feedback.** Treat feedback as a gift, not as a slap in the face. If you're blind to your flaws, you can't address them.

**Be open to fresh new ideas.** Solicit suggestions from everyone – not just those closest to you or of a certain rank. You never know where the next great idea will come from.

**Address your weak points.** Request positive *and* negative feedback. Positive comments feed your ego, negative ones enable you to improve your game.

**Get the scoop, *firsthand*.** Get your input directly from the horse's mouth rather than from secondhand sources. Surveys can be misinterpreted and don't always tell the *whole* story.

**Build *stronger* relationships.** Drop your defenses and let people get to know the real you. Even though walls keep bad people out, they never let good people in.

**Make *informed* decisions.** Encourage debate. Seek diverse opinions, embrace vigorous discussion, and examine all sides of an issue before taking a stand.

**Obtain *objective* information.** Seek the truth. Don't let people with a personal agenda or bias distort your views. Challenge the information you receive. Confirm its accuracy before you draw conclusions.

**Gain a *new* perspective.** See things in a new light. Don't allow mental filters to distort your thinking, influence your feelings, or impact your behavior. Have an open mind.

**Think for yourself.** Kick the tires before you get swept up by groupthink. Ask questions, scrutinize the facts, question the rationale, and examine whether people's intentions are honorable. Don't follow blindly.

**Venture outside your comfort zone.** Embrace positive change. Don't get complacent by succumbing to a "we've always done it this way" mentality.

## NEVER LIVE IN THE DARK AGAIN

How can you address weaknesses if you're blind to your flaws? How can you have meaningful relationships if you build walls around yourself? How will you know if your ideas are sound if you don't let people challenge them? The only difference between being uninformed and being misinformed is that one is *your* choice and the other is *theirs*.

*Some people hate the idea that others have a better idea.*

When you resist input, ignore feedback, select ideas from the chosen few, and live behind closed doors, you're going nowhere fast. You're stifling your ability to learn, destroying your ability to grow, and shutting your eyes to reality. Some folks believe that if you don't know your weaknesses, you don't have any. The reality is, closing your eyes to problems doesn't make them disappear. They're right under your nose even if you're unwilling to face them. Therefore, don't fear what you may learn about yourself, worry about what you don't. Are you living in the dark? It's time to see the light. :)

> PEOPLE STOP TRYING WHEN THERE'S NO BENEFIT FOR BEING EXCEPTIONAL AND NO CONSEQUENCE FOR BEING MEDIOCRE.

# ARE YOU SABOTAGING YOUR SUCCESS?

If I were a basketball coach, I'd recruit the best players. As a parent, I want the best teachers for my kids. If I had a serious illness, I'd seek out the best doctor. You have to wonder – why would anyone recruit a second-rate athlete, want a teacher who had lost their appetite for teaching, or retain an inexperienced doctor for a serious illness? That would be sabotaging your chance of success. You'd want the best possible outcome, wouldn't you?

Along the same lines, if you wanted to buy something, wouldn't you search for the best product at the least expensive price? Why would anyone pay top dollar or go out of their way to buy inferior goods? If this premise holds true, why would anyone tolerate mediocrity in their organization? They'd be sabotaging their success and ultimately causing their organization's demise.

## IS YOUR ORGANIZATION PROMOTING EXCELLENCE OR SABOTAGING ITS SUCCESS?

Organizations don't become excellent through magic. Leaders create an environment that's conducive to excellence. Here are 10 ways you might be sabotaging your organization's performance. Do these business practices sound familiar?

1. Folks get paid for *showing up* rather than for *producing results*.

2. *Who* you know becomes more important than *what* you do.
3. *Appearance* becomes more important than *substance*.
4. *Tenure* becomes more valued than *outcomes*.
5. Looking busy becomes more important than getting stuff done.
6. Performance evaluations are *subjective* rather than based on *objective* criteria.
7. Everyone is compensated *equally*, regardless of effort or performance.
8. Following the rules becomes more emphasized than doing the right thing.
9. People have responsibility, but no one is accountable.
10. Poor performance and dead weight are overlooked rather than addressed.

## IF YOU DON'T STRIVE FOR EXCELLENCE, YOU WON'T ACHIEVE IT

Some people say we shouldn't distinguish between exceptional and mediocre performance – everyone should receive a trophy. While that sounds great in theory, it doesn't work in practice.

*If you want excellence, you have to recognize and reward it. Period.* You can't grant the mediocre employee the same reward as the superstar; you can't give the average student the same grade as the terrific one; and you can't award the team that finishes last the same prize as the team that finishes first. Why? you ask. It reduces any incentive to strive for the best, to do your best, or to be the best.

> *People stop trying when there's no benefit for being exceptional and no consequence for being mediocre.*

Some people raise the issue of compassion – everyone should benefit *equally*. Ask yourself, did everyone make an equal investment? Did everyone make an equal effort? Did everyone produce equal results? The reason some folks deserve a greater reward is because they earned it.

*You don't get what you want; you get what you deserve.*

Therefore, if you want to promote excellence and still be compassionate, the answer isn't giving *everyone* a trophy regardless of how well they perform; rather, the answer is giving everyone *an equal opportunity* and providing them with *the tools to achieve success*. Therefore, everyone is free to decide how hard they're willing to work and the sacrifices they're prepared to make to achieve success.

*If you're not willing to make the commitment, don't complain about the outcome.*

This applies to organizations and individuals alike. If you want to achieve excellence, you must strive for it and settle for nothing less. We don't gain anything by lowering the bar so that *everyone* can clear it. That breeds mediocrity. There *is* a difference between winners and losers. In most cases, a winner did everything in their power to achieve success. The loser did not.

*When you tolerate mediocrity, you get more of it.*

Ask yourself whether you're more likely to get beaten by your competitors or by yourself. The truth is, your future will be determined more by *choice* than by *chance*. Are you sabotaging your success? :)

"

IT DOESN'T COST MORE TO STRIVE FOR EXCELLENCE, BUT IF YOU SETTLE FOR MEDIOCRITY, IT'LL COST YOU DEARLY.

"

# STEP UP YOUR GAME

Did you ever see someone step right over a piece of paper and not pick it up? You have to wonder: Did he see it or is he just plain lazy? The truth is, he probably also sees problems at work, yet fails to do anything about them. If that sounds familiar, it's time to step up your game.

Some people do what they have to, no more and no less. And if management doesn't specifically tell them to do something, it doesn't get done. Those folks feel that if they put in the hours, their work is done – regardless of whether they did a good job. The fact is, putting in the time doesn't cut it; getting the job done right is what counts.

Setting proper expectations can have a huge impact on an organization. The problem is that some leaders set the bar so low you could trip on it. When employees think that doing the bare minimum is acceptable, they get lazy. When employees take no pride in what they do, and when customers are treated like annoyances, that organization is in serious decline.

*When you tolerate mediocrity, you get more of it.*

## TAKE STEPS TO ACHIEVE EXCELLENCE

Here are 14 guideposts to step up your game:

**Raise the bar.** Don't settle for mediocrity. Be the best you can be… and then be a little better.

**Be your toughest critic.** Before challenging others, challenge yourself. If you're not proud, you're not done.

**Be proactive.** Don't wait for a complaint to act. If you see something wrong, fix it. The fact is, if you can do it right *after* being asked, you can do it right *before* being asked.

**Request feedback.** Get out of your office and get a reality check. Seek feedback *directly* from customers rather than receiving it second- or third-hand.

**Control your ego.** Treat negative feedback as a gift rather than as a slap in the face.

**Eliminate dissatisfaction.** Eliminate every area that dissatisfies customers because those are the reasons why customers leave. Then you can invest in delighting them.

**Anticipate needs.** Identify ways to add customer value. But remember to act on your findings. When you do nothing, nothing happens.

**Exceed expectations.** Some results, like accurate payroll checks, are expected. (You'll never win praise because your payroll is accurate.) Other results, such as going the extra mile, are often not expected. If you consistently exceed your customers' expectation levels and deliver greater value than they anticipated – you'll WOW people.

**Show what you're made of.** If you think you're doing your customers a "favor," you're in for a rude awakening. Competence, courtesy, reliability, and responsiveness are expected.

**Replicate success.** Turn great ideas into lasting success. When an improvement proves successful, institutionalize it so that it's not a one-time event.

**Measure what's important.** There's an old saying, "What gets measured gets done." Ask yourself, "What counts that we're not counting?"

**Empower your employees.** Encourage your employees to think for themselves and do what's in the best interests of their customers.

**Pay for performance.** Recognize and reward people for excellence, *not* for just showing up. Employees stop trying when there's no benefit for being exceptional and no consequence for being mediocre.

**Think long term.** Don't cut corners to save a penny. Invest in long-term customer relationships.

## MEDIOCRE BEHAVIOR IS A CHOICE

Some organizations permit their employees to do the absolute minimum. When leaders tolerate mediocrity, it's a cancer that spreads like wildfire. People stop trying, people stop caring, and people opt for what's easy rather than what's best. The truth is, some organizations have been operating this way for so long, they don't even realize they're becoming second rate. Don't let that happen to you.

*Taking down the "Out of Order" sign doesn't fix the problem.*

It's time to step up your game. When you expect exceptional behavior, you raise the bar for everyone; when you tolerate mediocrity, you lower the bar for everyone as well. Remember, mediocre behavior is a choice. And it starts with you. It doesn't cost more to strive for excellence, but if you settle for mediocrity, it'll cost you dearly. Always give 110%. It's the extra 10% that everyone remembers. :)

"

PEOPLE DON'T RESIST CHANGE; THEY RESIST *BEING* CHANGED.

"

# YOU CAN'T FORCE PEOPLE TO CHANGE

Did you ever try to change someone, but they were unwilling to do so? While you probably thought it would be easy, it was like pushing a boulder up a hill. You pushed, they resisted. You pushed harder, they resisted more. Frustrating. Right? What's wrong with them? you wondered. Why are they so stubborn? Why don't they see the situation like I do?

Did you ever consider that *you* may be part of the problem? The truth is, you can't *force* people to change.

The more you try to pressure or intimidate people to change, the less likely they are to do so. It doesn't matter whether you're a loving parent, a concerned friend, or a determined leader, you can't *force* people to change; they must be willing participants.

> *People don't resist change; they resist* being *changed.*

## GO AHEAD, MAKE ME

Let's step back and examine the forces at play. From your perspective, you think your guidance should be welcomed. After all, it's in their best interest. Right? So you expect compliance without delay. Of course, if change doesn't occur immediately, you lose patience. The truth is, while your recommendation may seem like a no-brainer to you, it's not that obvious to everyone else. After all, some folks are afraid of failure, while others fear the unknown or are simply set in their ways. That may explain why the harder you pushed, the harder they pushed back.

In addition, while some folks dig in their heels and cry foul, others go silent or shut down. While you think you've made headway, their silence says everything. The *best* you're likely to achieve is compliance. But you may also create animosity, anxiety, or resentment — or possibly damage trust along the way.

*Just because a person is silent doesn't mean there's no message.*

## A BETTER WAY TO INTRODUCE CHANGE

It doesn't matter whether you'd like someone to live a healthier lifestyle, break a bad habit, or implement a new business strategy — *forcing* people to change is a losing strategy. While it takes more time, *upfront*, to introduce change correctly, it'll save you a lot of aggravation in the long run.

*People change only when change is their choice.*

What can you do to encourage change? Here are 10 guideposts for your consideration:

**Establish intent.** Demonstrate that you understand everyone's situation and you're acting in their best interest.

**Build up trust.** People are more receptive to change if they trust and respect you rather than if change is demanded. Knowledge, experience, and credibility go a long way toward that end.

**Educate.** Share your knowledge rather than assuming that everyone's on the same page.

**Justify.** Great ideas don't have to be forced on people. Explain your assumptions and the rationale behind your thinking. In addition, allow time for people to absorb the information. Rushing people is heavy-handed.

**Involve.** Create an environment in which you *encourage* change rather than *demand* it. If you ram change down people's throats, *you'll* choke on the results.

**Create a sense of urgency.** Present the benefits of moving forward and the consequences of sitting idle.

**Set realistic expectations.** Adopt reasonable objectives rather than shooting for the moon.

**Build momentum.** Set achievable, short-term goals. Small wins will keep everyone motivated as you pursue your long-term targets.

**Establish ownership.** Encourage all involved to own the process and be accountable for results.

**Reinforce.** Set milestones and measure progress along the way. There is great truth to the saying, "What gets measured gets done."

## MAKE CHANGE THEIR CHOICE

If your *modus operandi* is abrupt, if you make threats or bully people to change, it's time for you to change your tune. Ask yourself four questions: "What's the case for change? How do people benefit? What's holding them back? And why should they begin today?" If you don't know the answers to these questions, neither will they. As Lao Tzu, the ancient Chinese philosopher, said, "A journey of a thousand miles begins with a single step." Encouraging change is a step in the right direction. :)

> YOU ARE WHAT YOU EAT AND THE INFORMATION THAT YOU DIGEST.

# PROTECT YOURSELF FROM BAD INFORMATION

There was a time when people believed the Earth was flat. They had good reason to feel that way, given that scholars and the masses were in complete agreement. While that may seem foolish now, some things you believe today may prove to be equally false tomorrow. The cause is bad information.

While you may *not* believe the Earth is flat, I can assure you that some of your thinking today is indeed flawed. It happens because you, like most people, often rely on *bad* information to shape your thoughts and opinions. As they say – garbage in, garbage out. The good news is that you can do something about it.

## YOU CAN'T BELIEVE EVERYTHING YOU HEAR (OR READ)

You are bombarded with information every day. You search the Internet, obtain advice from friends and family, read product reviews, hear the news on TV, and the list goes on. Ask yourself how much of what you hear or read from friends, colleagues, leaders, and so-called experts is accurate, objective, fair, and comprehensive. What if it's wrong? How does the information color your ideas and viewpoints?

The truth is, some of the information you receive is incorrect. Worse yet, some folks and organizations don't have your best interest at heart. They are dishonest and self-serving – and may even have a second agenda. Furthermore, while you may think that following the crowd is a safe bet, don't assume that the crowd has done their due diligence. In fact, they may be leading you right off a cliff.

*One or many believers don't determine the truth or untruth.*

## GARBAGE IN, GARBAGE OUT

There are specific things you can do to avoid getting burned by bad information. As a general rule of thumb, Ronald Reagan was right when he said, "Trust, but verify." The next time you search for information, read what's happening, receive input, get someone's opinion, or obtain a recommendation, consider the following:

Bad information can occur in three ways. First, the *method* that you use to obtain information may be haphazard. Second, the *source* may be bad. Last, the *information* itself may be flawed. Truth is not what it seems, but what it is.

Do you:

- Get information *secondhand* or from its *original source*?

- Subscribe to information that reinforces your *existing beliefs* or seek a *fresh perspective*?

- Accept everything at *face value* or view it with a healthy dose of *skepticism*?

- Listen to people because you *like them* or because they're *respected and reputable*?

- Determine whether the information is *opinion* or *fact*?

- Believe something is true because it's *well presented* or based on its *merit*?
- Determine whether the message is *one-sided* or presents *both sides* of the issue?
- Attack *opposing viewpoints* or try to see *the merit in others' opinions*?
- Accept advice *blindly* or ask *how the conclusion* was drawn?
- Assume *others know better* or trust *your own instincts*?

## FOOD FOR THOUGHT AND YOUR MIND

Although we live in a time in which information is plentiful and easily accessible, it's worthless if you don't harness it to your advantage. The key is to scrutinize the information that you receive – evaluating it for accuracy, honesty, objectivity, timeliness, and thoroughness. It also requires you to broaden your horizons, remain open to other peoples' thoughts and opinions, view things fairly and objectively, and encourage folks to challenge your thinking.

*An opinion is not a fact.*

If you're like most people these days, you're careful about what you put into your body. After all, the food that you consume impacts your energy, strength, brain power, and overall health. If you're that careful about consuming healthy food, shouldn't you be equally prudent about how you feed your mind? You are what you eat AND the information that you digest. Seize the opportunity to scrutinize this information carefully. Your thoughts, opinions, and beliefs hang in the balance. :)

"

# WHEN YOU SAY, 'I DON'T *HAVE* THE TIME,' WHAT YOU'RE REALLY SAYING IS 'I WON'T *MAKE* THE TIME.'

"

# HOW TO ADD MORE HOURS TO YOUR DAY

If you've ever cleaned out your attic, you know how much junk you can accumulate over time. Some of us keep stuff because we have the room, while others just can't be bothered to get rid of things. It got me thinking. If you won't clean up your clutter, how much of what *you do* is unnecessary as well? And what does that cost you?

We complain that we don't have time, that we juggle too many balls and have too many demands placed on us. Yet, why do we do unnecessary things that waste time? The fact is, we not only stockpile physical stuff, but we accumulate mental clutter as well. That adds stress, diverts valuable resources, and kills time that could be invested where it's needed most.

Think about the endless hours you spend following outdated rules and policies, searching for misplaced items, offering advice to those who don't want it, trying to change people who won't embrace it, struggling to control the uncontrollable, and of course, overthinking everything.

We can't help ourselves. We do these things because we live on autopilot, give in to bad habits, refuse to change, or simply don't have time to think. In any case, it's high time to reexamine our ways.

*If time is money, why don't people think twice before spending it?*

## DO YOU HAVE TIME TO KILL?

Time is one of your most precious resources. In fact, "I'm too busy" is another way of saying, "It's not a priority." Therefore, invest your time wisely. As Benjamin Franklin said, "Lost time is never found again." Do you spend long hours doing things that are:

**Useless.** Pointless. Ineffective. Totally unproductive.

> **Example:** Moving papers from one pile to another. Requesting advice with no intention of acting on it. Generating great ideas that collect dust on the shelf.

**Insignificant.** Trivial. Irrelevant. So minor that it's unworthy of your time and energy.

> **Example:** Making excuses. Holding grudges. Seeking revenge. Being envious. Feeling sorry for yourself. Worrying about the future or dwelling on the past.

**Unneeded.** Not helpful. Not required. Completely unnecessary.

> **Example:** Creating rules without insisting that they be followed. Holding *regularly scheduled* meetings – with nothing to say.

**Redundant.** Excessive. Overlapping. A complete duplication of effort.

> **Example:** Reinventing the wheel. Repeating mistakes without learning from them. Working at cross-purposes. Doing things over rather than doing them right the first time.

**Unwanted.** Unsolicited. Unwelcomed. Totally undesired.

> **Example:** Looking over people's shoulders. Needing to be right – all the time.

**Expendable.** Wasteful. Optional. A total misuse of your limited resources.

> **Example:** Spending an hour to save a dollar. Starting *many* things without finishing *anything*. Gathering facts and then ignoring them.

**Extraneous.** Irrelevant. Unconnected. Completely unrelated to the task.

> **Example:** Playing politics. Complaining without offering a solution. Keeping busy for the sake of keeping busy. Talking behind someone's back. Making people jump through hoops – to show them who's boss.

## MAKE UP FOR LOST TIME

Some people are too busy to find ways to save time. They think the best way to buy time is to do things faster. They believe the more they rush…the more gets done. That's like trying to fill a bucket that has holes. They think if you pour water fast enough, you'll fill the bucket. But plugging the holes, first, is a lot smarter and certainly more productive. I'm sure you have a to-do list. Start by eliminating unnecessary activities that are hijacking your day. Subtracting from your list of priorities is as important as adding to it.

*When was the last time you created a "don't-do" list?*

We all have 24 hours in a day. But each of us spends our time differently. When you say, "I don't *have* the time," what you're really saying is "I won't *make* the time." Therefore, next time you say you don't have enough time in the day, remember it's not that you don't have enough time. You choose to spend it doing something else.  :)

"

MEASURE PROGRESS —
NOT THE TIME THAT
YOU'RE WORKING.

"

# DISTRACTIONS, DISRUPTIONS, AND OTHER TIME-WASTERS

Did you ever ask yourself, where did the day go? Even though you had high hopes of getting stuff done, you didn't clear your plate...again. Despite the fact that you worked tirelessly throughout the day, time simply got away from you. Sound familiar? It doesn't matter if you're at the office or doing chores at home, you have only so many hours in the day. If your time is spent efficiently, you're home free. But distractions and disruptions can easily hijack your day. (Ugh!)

While it's easy to blame the hijacking on interruptions, fire drills, and problems that came out of left field, the real reason most stuff doesn't get done *isn't* due to external forces – it's your own doing. In other words, we have no one to blame except ourselves.

*Those who waste the most time are usually
the first to complain of having too little.*

## SELF-IMPOSED TIME-WASTERS

Here are 10 ways that distractions sidetrack you from getting things done:

**Interruptions.** Some people look up every time a new email or text arrives. Or they gossip with friends who aren't busy – even though *they* are.

**Avoidances.** Some folks do *easy things* first, even though they're unimportant. They also do stuff they *enjoy* rather than things that have to get done.

**Disorganization.** Some people spend valuable time searching for computer files or items they've misplaced. It never occurs to them to clean up their act.

**Procrastination.** Some folks spend much of their day putting out fires when many of those problems could've been addressed when they were small. Do you spend more time lighting fires or putting them out?

**Emotion.** Some people spend precious time reliving the past or worrying about the future. Do you spend more time stressing about work or doing it?

**Mindset.** Some folks add unnecessary things to their to-do list and then complain about how overwhelmed they are. How about subtracting some items?

**Emergencies.** Some people let others hijack their day. Just because it says URGENT doesn't necessarily mean it's important. Poor planning on your part shouldn't constitute an emergency for others.

**Attention span.** Some folks check their social media feeds, respond to comments, and laugh at jokes texted to them. They let themselves get interrupted all day long.

**Multitasking.** Some people think that looking busy makes them more productive.

**Perfection.** Some folks strive for perfection rather than excellence. They never seem to get stuff done.

*Those who begin things, but never complete them, accomplish nothing.*

## 10 POWERFUL WAYS TO REDUCE DISTRACTIONS AND REMAIN ON COURSE

**Identify distractions.** You can't address distractions if you're unaware of them.

**Prioritize.** It's less important to get *everything* done than to make sure you get the *right things* done.

**Plan your week; schedule your day.** Determine your priorities for the week and set daily goals. Make sure to review your activity and apply lessons learned each day.

**Focus.** Tackle one thing at a time – single tasking.

**Take scheduled breaks.** Schedule *planned* breaks to check voicemail, email, and texts, as well as to return calls.

**Minimize distractions:**

> **Do not disturb.** If people know you're swamped or on a tight deadline – beforehand – they're less inclined to hijack your time.
>
> **Learn to say "no."** It's nice to be needed. But don't try to make everyone happy at the expense of your own needs.
>
> **Delegate.** Increase your productivity by delegating tasks to others. In addition, if you can't satisfy a request, suggest an alternative way of satisfying it.
>
> **Clean your clutter.** Declutter. If you know things distract you, put them away. As they say, "Out of sight, out of mind." Furthermore, clear your mental clutter too. Meditation and/or exercise will increase your productivity.
>
> **Prioritize what NOT to do.** Know the things that distract you most and eliminate or minimize those activities.
>
> **Control your technology.** Set constraints on technology use.

**Set artificial deadlines.** There is great truth to Parkinson's Law: "Work expands to fill the time available for its completion." Therefore, create artificial deadlines to ensure progress.

**Measure advancement.** Measure progress – not the time that you're working.

**Reiterate your goals.** Review your goals on an ongoing basis to ensure that you're still on course.

**Be disciplined.** If you don't get something done, it's not that you didn't have time; you just chose to spend it doing something else. :)

"

**PEOPLE THINK GOOD TIMES WILL LAST FOREVER... UNTIL THEY DON'T.**

"

# GOOD TIMES DON'T LAST FOREVER

You can't see around the bend. For that reason, the only way to predict the future is to study the past or extrapolate what we know to be true today. But what if revolutionary changes occur or external events blindside you? The fact is, when times are good, you think they'll continue forever. But statistically speaking, that'll never happen.

*People think good times will last forever…until they don't.*

When was the last time you found yourself saying, "No one's going to knock us out of first place. My job's totally secure." Or "My health is always good." How would you feel if one of those scenarios changed tomorrow? The truth is, there are things you can do to prepare for that eventuality – and you should. But you'll never truly know what it's like to face a personal setback, or how you'll actually respond, until you face tough times.

## LET THE GOOD TIMES ROLL, BUT BE SMART ABOUT IT

There may be very little you can do to prevent tough times, but you can control the way you respond to them. Give it some thought before it happens. It's easier to be rational when you're not emotional. Here are eight guideposts to help you prepare for hard times:

**Be realistic.** Don't become complacent by believing that good times will last forever.

**Be practical.** Problems are best addressed before they arise. Don't wait for a fire to locate the exits.

**Be positive.** Surround yourself with positive and supportive people.

**Be proactive.** Think about what you'd do if you were faced with tough times. For example, take steps to remain healthy, reduce overhead costs, and expand your social network.

**Be cautious.** Hedge your *bets* to protect your downside. If you place all your eggs in one basket, any fall will be a messy one.

**Be humble.** Remain grounded. Don't let success go to your head. Achieving success is hard; staying successful is even harder.

**Be accountable.** Own the problem. Don't waste precious time and energy making excuses or casting blame. Move forward rather than dwelling in the past.

**Be determined.** As Richard M. Nixon said, "A man is not finished when he is defeated. He is finished when he quits."

## HAVE YOU EVER BEEN TESTED?

It's easy to feel invincible when times are good, but don't get pompous and lazy and forget all the hard work that made you successful. In short, you can get lulled into a false sense of security and may even start taking things for granted. But then when reality hits, you're grossly unprepared for the situation that befalls you.

*It's easier to maintain momentum than to rebuild it once it's lost.*

This won't happen to you, you say? Life is long. The possibility of facing a setback one day is inevitable – so be forewarned. There will be times when you can push through a temporary setback, while other times you'll have to live with the cards that were dealt to you. The key is that exceptional people don't shun tests of their strength and determination – they relish them.

*Challenges are not the measure of their greatness, but rather the pathway to it.*

Some people quit – and throw in the towel. Others reach deep down into their soul and rise to the occasion. In any case, your true character will become clear when times get tough. And how you choose to respond to the challenge will say volumes about who you really are. Do you get frustrated and complain "Why me?" – or do you face the setback head-on with grace? Do you take your frustration out on the people around you or do you view them as a pillar of strength and great comfort? Do you view your setback as an opportunity to learn or are you too pigheaded to adjust your ways in the future?

When you are tested – and prove you can rise to the occasion – you'll be able to wear your response as a badge of honor. You can take great pride knowing that your backbone was tested and that you came through it with flying colors. Let the good times roll.  :)

"

**LIFE ISN'T ABOUT THE NUMBER OF UPS AND DOWNS THAT YOU EXPERIENCE, BUT HOW YOU DEAL WITH THEM.**

"

## HOW WELL DO YOU HANDLE LIFE'S UPS AND DOWNS?

If you play a competitive sport, you know what it's like to experience a crushing defeat and still have to mentally prepare yourself for the next game. If you're lucky, you also know what it's like to trounce a stronger team and prepare for your next opponent – without letting success go to your head. Even a good day can feel like a roller-coaster ride.

Face the facts. Over the course of your lifetime, you'll be confronted with good times and bad. If you maintain a level head, it'll work to your advantage. But if you *overreact* to situations – by getting overconfident or exceedingly gloomy – you'll be making it harder on yourself.

That doesn't mean you shouldn't take the time to celebrate a win or mourn a loss. But there's a difference between giving yourself a well-deserved pat on the back versus getting cocky. At the same time, failing one time, or even several times, doesn't make you a failure any more than losing one game makes you a loser. So get over it.

*If you say something to yourself often enough,*
*you may start to believe it.*

## SEVEN WAYS TO RIDE LIFE'S UPS AND DOWNS

The way that you respond to situations says a lot about you and will ultimately determine your success and happiness.

**Be in control.** Some things are beyond your control. Then again, you *do* have control over how you respond to each situation.

**Manage your expectations.** Every day won't be bright and sunny. If life were a bed of roses, you'd still need to avoid the thorns.

**Don't overreact.** Don't believe everything you think. When things go well, don't assume good times will last forever. When things go wrong, don't think the world is coming to an end. Like most things, the truth lies somewhere in-between.

**Keep things in perspective.** Don't take things to extremes. It's never helpful to be overconfident or to punish yourself for disappointments. If you build a lifestyle based on the good old times lasting forever, you may be in for a rude awakening. What's more, if you beat yourself up over one failed effort, you can turn *one* unfortunate situation into lasting damage to your self-confidence.

**Cut yourself some slack.** Don't take losses personally. Separate the incident from your self-worth. Mistakes don't make you a failure, but beating yourself up makes you feel like one.

**Live and learn.** Do you view failure as a slap in the face or as an opportunity to learn? The difference between a stepping-stone and a stumbling block is the way in which you approach it.

**Be patient.** Nothing lasts forever. When you're in the throes of a bad patch, a minute can feel like a lifetime. It helps to remember that this too shall pass – it takes a rain shower to create a rainbow.

## HOW DO YOU HANDLE LIFE'S UPS AND DOWNS?

Life isn't about the number of ups and downs that you experience, but how you deal with them. You can let success go to your head and become complacent. Or you can remain grounded and check your ego at the door. You can get angry, feel sorry for yourself, and cast blame during tough times. Or you can stay calm, remain true to your values, and look for a trace of blue in the dark skies ahead.

*Life is filled with ups and downs,*
*so make the most of the in-betweens.*

You have a choice. You can let yourself be knocked around during the roller-coaster ride we call life or you can accept the highs and lows in stride. The choice that you make will not only affect your mental health and success rate, but it'll also determine your happiness. The difference between a winner and an also-ran isn't always that the loser fell on hard times; it's how the loser faced the adversity. Win or lose, it's up to you. Enjoy the ride.  :)

"

PROBLEMS ARE
BEST ADDRESSED
BEFORE THEY ARISE.

"

# READ THIS BEFORE IT'S TOO LATE

In the 1950s, "Made in Japan" was synonymous with shoddy merchandise. In the decades that followed, the Japanese not only shed that stigma, they became a manufacturing powerhouse. How did they achieve that feat and why should you care?

In essence, different philosophies produced different actions. While the Japanese created business practices and processes to achieve quality excellence *before* the manufacturing process took place, U.S. companies did the opposite. They added quality control inspectors *afterward* to find defective products. The rest is history. Japanese products took the world by storm. What can we learn from this lesson? And how can you apply this principle to your daily life?

How often do you fail to do things properly in the first place and find yourself forced to fix them afterward? Think about it...we fail to plan upfront and then act surprised when things go astray; we treat people poorly and are obliged to mend relationships later; we do things quickly and are forced to do them again. Does that sound familiar?

*Problems are best addressed before they arise.*

## DO IT RIGHT THE FIRST TIME

Here are 15 ways to spend a little time beforehand to save yourself a lot of aggravation afterward:

**Think before you act.** Determine the best way to do something before you begin. Ready, fire, aim is a recipe for disaster.

**Make a commitment.** Most things in life require sacrifice. If you're not willing to make the commitment *beforehand*, don't complain about the outcome.

**Prepare contingency plans.** Things rarely go according to plan. Ask yourself "what-if" questions. When planning life's journey, always have an alternate route.

**Protect your downside.** Many people focus on upside potential while disregarding the downside. Protect yourself in case of a calamity.

**Think before you speak.** Think before you open your mouth. You can't undo what's been said.

**Invest in your relationships.** It's easier to treat people properly than to repair broken relationships.

**Make your kids self-sufficient.** Give your kids a solid education, instill good values, and set them free. As Frederick Douglass, the American statesman, said, "It is easier to build strong children than to repair broken men."

**Embrace a healthy lifestyle.** You can't live an unhealthy lifestyle and expect a healthy outcome.

**Live within your means.** Keeping up with the Joneses is a high price to pay. When you run out of money, stop buying.

**Listen to your conscience.** It's easier to do what's right than to defend your actions after an indiscretion.

**Plan for the inevitable.** Some things in life shouldn't come as a surprise. Don't wait until it's too late to save for your kid's education or your retirement.

**Make your money work for you.** You work so hard to earn money. If you don't take the time to invest it properly, it won't work for you. In addition, save for a rainy day. Don't wait for a fire to locate the exits.

**Manage your resources with care.** We all have limited resources. Establish priorities before you waste your resources on frivolous things.

**Create good karma.** If your thoughts, intentions, and deeds are heartfelt and beneficial to others, they'll come back full circle – like a boomerang. The same holds true for negative behavior.

**Live without regrets.** Make your priorities a priority. Life isn't a dress rehearsal.

## SPEED AT ALL COSTS CAN BE COSTLY

We shoot from the hip, talk before we think, and run full speed ahead before we know where we're going. And then we act surprised when those actions come back to bite us one day. The truth is, if you spend a little time upfront, you'll save a lot of aggravation on the back end.

*Do it right the first time or be forced to do it again, later.*

You may be thinking the world is moving at light speed and you don't want to get left behind. Ask yourself whether speed at all costs is helping your efforts or holding you back. While it may feel good being busy, it's taking a toll on you by creating inefficiency, waste, stress, and even regret. Stop for a moment and think – before it's too late. :)

"

DON'T COUNT
YOUR FRIENDS —
COUNT *ON* THEM.

"

# IS YOUR FRIEND REALLY AN ACQUAINTANCE?

There are folks you've known for many years, had their kids over to play with your kids, spent time with them at work, and you may have been on the receiving end of a favor or two. Does that make them a friend – or an acquaintance? You may be asking yourself, why does that matter? The fact is, if you don't know the true meaning of friendship, can *you* be a *real* friend?

## FRIENDSHIP IS LIKE MARRIAGE

Good friends place a high value on their relationships and actively invest in their friendships. According to Ambrose Bierce, the American writer, an acquaintance is "A person whom we know well enough to borrow from, but not well enough to lend to." As you review the list below, ask yourself, "How many *true* friends do I have?"

- You bring out the best in your friend and make him feel good about himself.

- You're delighted for your friend's happiness and never envious of her success.

- You put your friend's needs ahead of your own and know that your kindness will be reciprocated one day. But you never keep score. Your joy comes from giving.

- You're willing to do anything for your friend — even when it's inconvenient.

- If your friend needs something, you jump right in, but you know when to back off and never force your will on him.

- You make your friend feel at ease — no judging. Your friend can be herself with no need to put on a show.

- You're happy just to be in your friend's company. You don't need to be entertained to have a good time.

- You're comfortable sharing your innermost thoughts and feelings with your friend.

- You're also good at being a sounding board — being all ears if required.

- You don't sugarcoat bad news. You tell it like it is — even if it hurts.

- Your friend's behavior is so reliable and consistent, you can predict his words and actions. That strengthens trust between you.

- You know your friend like the back of your hand. In fact, you know each other so well, it feels like you can communicate without talking.

- Even though you and your friend don't always see eye-to-eye, you respect your friend's opinions. True friends fiercely debate issues and still walk away as friends.

- You have total faith in your friend. You watch her back – in good times and bad – and never have to second-guess her motives.

- Time and distance have little if any bearing on your relationship. You can be separated from each other and then pick up right back where you left off.

- You are very protective of your relationship. You'd never take your friendship for granted or do anything to jeopardize it.

- Last, but not least, you share common *interests* and *values*. Principles form the heart of every successful relationship and can ultimately determine its success.

## REAL FRIENDSHIPS ARE PRICELESS

Some folks gloat over the number of friends they have and treat popularity as a gauge of self-worth. Others measure the depth of their friendships, knowing that relationships are the real treasure in life. The bottom line is, don't *count your friends – count on them.* While the number of friends may feed your ego, it will never satisfy your heart.

The question remains, can you develop meaningful relationships with a zillion friends? Only you know the answer for sure. Friendships require significant investment and sacrifice. But there's nothing more rewarding than a true friendship. As Ralph Waldo Emerson said, "The only way to have a friend is to be one." Treat your friendships like a valuable treasure. Possessions wear out; relationships are forever.  :)

> JUST BECAUSE ONE PERSON COMMITS A CRIME DOESN'T MEAN YOU SHOULD THROW THE WHOLE TOWN IN JAIL.

# HAVE YOU EVER BEEN BETRAYED?

Did you ever put someone on a pedestal because she *said* all the right things, only to learn that her *actions* spoke otherwise? Did you ever associate with someone you thought was bighearted, only to learn that he just cared about himself? Did you ever form a business relationship with someone you felt was trustworthy, only to discover that she was underhanded and deceitful? If you put your trust in someone and that person proves unworthy, it's like being dropped on your head, BIG time.

It's one thing to be deceived by a distant acquaintance and quite another to be betrayed by a friend or associate you've put your utmost faith in. That's devastating. It can make you feel regretful, insecure, and even violated.

> *Trust takes a long time to develop,*
> *but it can be lost in the blink of an eye.*

## HOW TO RESPOND TO BETRAYAL

If you're a victim of this kind of transgression, you might think "How could I have been so stupid to trust him? Why didn't I see the warning signs?" Who would have thought that someone you trusted would stab you in the back? With friends like that, who needs enemies?

Incidents like these can lead to self-doubt and scornful mistrust. "I wonder if there are more people like this in my life," you may think. As Warren Buffett said, "There's never just one cockroach in the kitchen." That may cause you to withdraw or to build a wall to protect yourself from being hurt again. Some people may even go to extremes — and lose faith in mankind.

Before we go that far, it's important to distinguish between two kinds of indiscretions — those beyond the perpetrator's control versus those that are deliberate. For the most part, you may be forgiving and not find your trust shaken if someone makes an honest mistake — nobody's perfect. On the other hand, when improper actions are intentional — a conscious assault on you — your trust is undermined and forgiving takes more effort.

## FOOL ME ONCE, SHAME ON YOU...

Does the perpetrator deserve a second chance? It's reasonable to think that if the culprit betrayed you once, he may do it again. But you be the judge. At a minimum, he owes you an apology. Period. If you don't receive one, his saying *nothing* says *everything*. If you do receive an apology, it shouldn't be just a knee-jerk reaction acknowledging that he hurt you. It should be a statement of remorse with an explicit promise that it won't happen again. It's also important that those words are coupled with a real desire to change. In any case, trust but verify.

*Trust is like Humpty Dumpty...once broken,
it's hard to put the pieces back together.*

What's the lesson here? First, the biggest loser is the offender. He may think he's fooling the world, but he's only kidding himself. If he violated your trust, the odds are he's doing it to others. That kind of behavior will never lead to meaningful relationships – his loss. Second, you can't control people's actions, but you can control your reaction to their behavior. There's no doubt that when someone violates your trust, you may feel hurt and victimized. But don't let your feelings make a bad situation worse. While it's understandable to mistrust *someone*, don't lose faith in *everyone*. The fact is, just because one person commits a crime doesn't mean you should throw the whole town in jail.

There are a lot of decent and honorable people in the world. Rise above the situation by continuing to put your faith in the power of trust. You will benefit from one of life's greatest gifts while disreputable people fritter that opportunity away. Furthermore, learn from their mistakes: If you want to be deemed trustworthy, earn it every day, and never prove yourself unworthy of someone's faith. Trust is like blood pressure. It's silent, vital to good health, and if abused, it can be deadly. :)

"

CHANGE IS GOOD —
IF IT'S IN THE
RIGHT DIRECTION.

"

# DO YOU REMEMBER THE GOOD OLD DAYS?

Change has been sweeping the globe, and it has had a profound impact on our lives. Maybe it's time to see where change has taken us. After all, change is good – if it's in the right direction. Do you remember the good old days when:

- It was cool to love your country.
- A cell phone wasn't considered part of a table setting.
- A news anchor was the most trusted man in America.
- Time off was time off.
- Parents reprimanded their kids without getting reprimanded.
- Celebrities became famous for the roles they took on, not the clothes they took off.
- Spam was food.
- You didn't count your friends; you counted *on* them.
- Kids used to whine. Now grown-ups do.
- Hard work was a celebrated virtue.
- Teachers spent more time answering student, rather than parent, questions.

- The book *1984* was science fiction.
- Preparing dinner didn't require a phone.
- Doing something illegal was against the law.
- Disrespecting your elders had consequences.
- Sunday morning was reserved for church.
- PC meant computer.
- Free speech was talked up.
- A penny bought something.
- Rewards went to the most deserving.
- Politicians were considered role models.
- Your mouth was washed out with soap for using foul language.
- People talked *to* each other, not *over* each other.
- You supported your local Mom-and-Pop store.
- We *wrote* love letters rather than *texting* them.
- Teachers were teachers and politicians were politicians.
- Traditions were honored.
- You only checked for mail one time per day.
- Sears was a household name.
- Lebanon was a tourist destination.
- Children didn't need a license to open a lemonade stand.
- Holidays were celebrated, not attacked.
- Bad news traveled slower.
- Veterans Day was more than a sale day.
- People were too proud to accept handouts.
- Snowflakes fell out of the sky.

- Success wasn't frowned upon.
- Children entertained themselves.
- Raising kids was considered a full-time job.
- People were *not* offended when you said, "Merry Christmas."
- Stepping up meant raising *your* hand, not volunteering someone else.
- You *earned* your trophy.
- Politicians ran for office not *from* their constituents.
- Face-to-face conversations weren't made via phone.
- Kids' sports were not a fierce competition.
- Doctors made house calls.
- Personal notes were handwritten, not typed.
- People said it doesn't pay to exercise. (Now they're paying for it.)
- You didn't *expect* rewards, you *earned* them.
- *Little House on the Prairie* and *The Cat in the Hat* were considered children's classics.
- Christmas was less about presents and more about *being* present.
- Holding the door for someone was a welcomed gesture.
- Nobody had all the answers. (Now everyone does.)
- Kids recited the Pledge of Allegiance in school.
- Airline travel was considered luxurious.

This isn't a plea to return to the past. It's an appeal to pause.... Just because it's new doesn't make it better. If change isn't making things better, it's time for change. Life doesn't happen *to* us. It's created *by* us. :)

"

IF WE GIVE
OUR CHILDREN
EVERYTHING,
WE DEPRIVE THEM
OF ASPIRATIONS.

"

# 25 WAYS TO SCREW UP YOUR KIDS

Being a good parent isn't for the faint of heart. It'll test your wisdom, challenge your stamina, and defy your patience. But even though you're not paid to be on your toes 24/7, it's the most rewarding job in the world.

As parents, we want the very best for our kids: to lead happy, healthy, and productive lives. We want our kids to live up to their potential, to grow up to be decent human beings, and to contribute back to society. But, although these goals are very admirable, getting across the finish line isn't always easy.

Even though there's always been a debate between nurture and nature, the fact remains that bringing a child into this world will always be an incredible responsibility.

*Our future is dependent on our kids.*
*And the future of your children is dependent on you.*

## ARE YOU HELPING OR HURTING YOUR KIDS?

The truth of the matter is that parents aren't perfect – regardless of what some may say. Here are 25 ways to screw up your kids:

1. Undervalue education.
2. Make everything about money.
3. Rarely discipline.
4. Be unavailable.
5. Teach them to hate.
6. Belittle hard work.
7. Never say "no."
8. Allow them to shrug off responsibility.
9. Fight their battles for them.
10. Buy their love.
11. Overlook bad behavior.
12. Make them dependent.
13. Tolerate mediocrity.
14. Push them too hard.
15. Fail to set limits.
16. Take your problems out on them.
17. Give them everything they want.
18. Place conditions on your love.
19. Allow them to disrespect others.
20. Strip them of their confidence.
21. Fail to impart good values.
22. Teach them to be selfish.
23. Make life too easy for them.
24. Serve as a poor role model.
25. Abandon parental responsibility.

## GIVE YOUR KIDS THE GREATEST GIFT

There is a common thread among the 25 items.

If you want your kids to be happy, successful, and well-adjusted adults, it requires your time, your dedication, and your love (with a touch of luck). Being a good parent is hard work. If you don't make the effort to nurture your kids, don't expect it to happen magically.

*Having kids is not the same as being a parent.*

If you want your kids to possess strong moral character, it's critical to live *your* life that way. While you can lecture them until you're blue in the face, the best way to teach your children to be honorable is to lead by example. Period!

*Watch your children grow and they will teach you what you've taught them.*

If you want your kids to be confident, learn important life skills, and have a strong self-image, don't overprotect them or make their life unrealistically easy.

*If we give our children everything, we deprive them of aspirations.*

While it's tough to say "no" or to sit on the sidelines in the face of adversity, prepare them for the real world by teaching them to become self-reliant. That means promoting the value of hard work, making good choices, and insisting that they accept responsibility for their actions. Therefore, if you want to give your kids the greatest gift of all, give them a good education, instill good values, inspire them, and set them free. Behind every good kid are parents or caregivers who understand the importance of raising them that way. :)

"

GOODNESS IS A
BRIGHT FLAME WITHIN
YOU. USE IT TO LIGHT
UP THE WORLD.

"

# A MESSAGE TO GRADUATES: HERE'S THE BEST-KEPT SECRET

If you were granted one wish, what would it be? Some graduates might opt for riches beyond their wildest dreams, while others might select something practical or choose to pay it forward to a loved one. What if this scenario wasn't a fairy tale and you could actually make your wish come true?

The truth is, you can achieve anything you want in life as long as you work hard and are willing to make the commitment. While that may sound simple, it's not. The fact is, everything has its price. It not only takes effort and dedication, but there are serious tradeoffs in the process. That's because every time you say "yes" to one thing, you're also saying "no" to another. (Unless you can be in two places at the same time.) So be careful what you wish for. The last thing you'd want is to achieve your dreams but be saddled with regrets.

## DON'T LET OBSTACLES STAND IN YOUR WAY

Before you begin your journey, here's a word of caution. There are several obstacles that will stand in your way – some are beyond your control while other impediments are self-inflicted. Your job is to circumvent them.

Here are six barriers to success:

**Indifference.** Some people never get out of the starting gate because they don't know what they want. While that's fine at first, don't make it a lifelong habit.

**Laziness.** Some folks don't want to work hard, so they fail to make the required effort.

**Entitlement.** Some people expect everything to be handed to them on a silver platter. That's ridiculous. The world doesn't owe you anything. The sooner you learn that lesson, the better off you'll be.

**Hesitation.** Some graduates doubt themselves, or worse yet, let people talk them out of pursuing their dreams.

**Inaction.** Some people fail because they're all talk. Dreams, unlike eggs, don't hatch from sitting on them.

**Weakness.** Some folks quit when they hit their first obstacle. Face it – life isn't all roses and rainbows. Show some grit.

## STOP WISHING AND START DOING

**Be resilient.** Remain positive. If you believe you can't, you won't.

**Be brave.** The next time someone says, "The odds are against you," remember: If you don't try, you forfeit the opportunity.

**Be accountable.** Take ownership of your choices rather than relinquishing that responsibility to others.

**Be focused.** It's hard to be good at *one* thing, much less *everything*. The fact is, trying to be excellent at everything leads to mediocrity.

**Be strong-minded.** Don't be deterred by roadblocks. The difference between a stepping-stone and a stumbling block is in the way you approach it.

## ONE LAST THING...

When you're granted one wish, your first inclination might be to ask for expensive jewelry, a fancy car, or even a luxury yacht. While extravagant indulgences may make other folks green with envy, these riches aren't what they're cracked up to be.

The fact is, we place artificial demands on ourselves that undermine our happiness. These demands force us to work harder and harder to cross a finish line that keeps moving. And then one day we'll sit back, or more likely collapse in exhaustion, wondering what we've gained from this frenetic race called life. And in those moments of retrospection, will we really regret that we didn't get the most glamorous things in life? Or will we ponder our failed relationships – the feelings left unshared with someone we love, or the precious time we lost with our children?

> *Goodness is a bright flame within you.*
> *Use it to light up the world.*

There *is* a difference between success and happiness. Rather than wishing for power, money, and status to impress others – pursue the life that makes *you* and your loved ones happy. Once you identify that goal, make the commitment and pursue it with passion. As Michael Jordan said, "Some people want it to happen, some wish it would happen, others make it happen." In the end, dreams come true not because you *wished* them to come true, but because you *made* them come true. :)

"

**DREAMS, UNLIKE EGGS, DON'T HATCH FROM SITTING ON THEM.**

"

# IF YOU HAD THREE WISHES, WHAT WOULD THEY BE?

If you had three wishes, what would they be? Would you benefit yourself or help others? Would you advance your career, health, or financial well-being, or would you further your social, emotional, or spiritual needs? Would you blow through your wishes right away, or would you hold a few in reserve?

You may be thinking this is a silly exercise, but your answers can be quite telling. For example, what do your wishes say about your priorities? Do they focus on possessions or enhance your relationships? What do your wishes say about your current situation versus your ultimate goals? Are your wishes far-fetched or clearly within your grasp?

*Dreams, unlike eggs, don't hatch from sitting on them.*

## DON'T YOU WISH

If your wishes are things that you long for, what's holding you back? Here are 10 guidelines to consider. Are you:

**Spreading yourself too thin?** If everything's a priority, then nothing's a priority. You don't have unlimited resources and can't be in two places at the same time.

**Waiting for things to happen by magic?** If your wishes haven't become a reality to date, what makes you think sitting around waiting is productive?

**Afraid of failure?** If you stop focusing on all the reasons why you *can't* do something, you just may surprise yourself when you see what you *can* do.

**More talk than action?** When you do nothing, nothing happens. It's that simple.

**Unwilling to make the commitment?** Everything worth striving for requires a certain level of sacrifice to achieve success. If you're not willing to make the commitment, don't complain about the outcome.

**Trying too hard to please others?** Make *your* priorities a priority. If you're trying too hard to please others, you may fail to satisfy your *own* needs.

**Intimidated by the work required?** You don't get what you want; you get what you deserve. Very few things come to those who don't work hard. When you work your tail off for something, it isn't luck.

**Doing things for the wrong reasons?** Stop trying to keep up with the Joneses. If you're spending your whole life chasing rainbows, you'll never catch up with your dreams.

**Focusing on the wrong things?** Keep things in perspective. Material possessions get old and wear out. Memories last forever.

**Waiting for the perfect time to act?** There's never a perfect time. Avoid regrets and do it now.

## MAKE YOUR WISHES COME TRUE

You may not have the opportunity to make three wishes, but you can still make your dreams come true. If you want your life story to have a happy ending, don't pursue your wishes hesitantly; go after your dreams with gusto. As Christopher Reeve, the American actor, said, "So many of our dreams at first seem impossible, then they seem improbable, and then, when we summon the will, they soon become inevitable."

*A wish without action is merely a pipe dream.*

Some people have incredible ability but fail to live up to their true potential. They say their dreams are out of reach as an excuse not to try. Others want the rewards but are unwilling to make the effort. Although some of your dreams may be tough to attain, most things in life are achievable IF you're willing to make the sacrifice. That requires hard work, commitment, and unyielding determination — don't let people convince you otherwise. It's your life, your journey, and it will ultimately be your prize. The alternative is waiting around till you're granted three wishes. Dream on! :)

"

PERSONAL BRANDING IS LESS A MARKETING EXERCISE THAN IT IS BECOMING THE BEST PERSON YOU CAN BE.

"

# WHAT'S YOUR PERSONAL BRAND WORTH?

It's a brand-new world. In the past, employees remained with their employers for life. Today, the Bureau of Labor Statistics cites that full-time employees will average 11.7 jobs from ages 18 to 48. Additionally, some folks act as free agents who do project work for any organization willing to retain their services. For that reason, whether you serve as a full-time or a contract employee, it's critical to build your personal brand to remain marketable.

That begs the question, what steps should you take to build your personal brand? What's the most effective way to stand out among your peers? What's the best way to get the word out? The fact is: Take a hands-off approach at your own peril!

## 10 STEPS TO MAKE A NAME FOR YOURSELF

Whether you're a full-time employee or a freelancer for several organizations, it's critical to develop a personal brand that showcases the knowledge, expertise, and value that you provide. Your brand will serve you well throughout your career. Here are 10 steps to make a name for yourself:

1. Find your *niche*.
2. Create a clear *value proposition*.
3. Develop a narrative that *distinguishes you* from others.

4. Identify *challenging, thought-provoking, noteworthy* projects that you want to undertake.
5. Establish credibility by doing *cutting-edge work* for *world-class organizations.*
6. Generate a track record of *proven results.*
7. Marshal a cadre of influential *movers and shakers* who mentor you and are willing to *sing your praises.*
8. Encourage *word-of-mouth* publicity that demonstrates your worth.
9. Create content that showcases your *knowledge* and *experience.*
10. Network, network, *network.*

## GOOD NEWS TRAVELS FAST

The bottom line is to create a buzz that you've been *retained by the best organizations,* to *address tough* – rather than run-of-the-mill – *challenges,* and have amassed *an impressive record of proven results.*

That will trigger others to think:

"If you're *good enough* for them, you're good enough for me."

"If you did that *type of work* for them, you can obviously handle this work for me."

"If you *delivered results* like that for them, I'll never lose sleep if you work for me."

Whoa. Wait a minute!

## IS PERSONAL BRANDING SIMPLY A PR ACTIVITY, OR...?

If you think personal branding is *entirely* a marketing and public relations activity, you've got it *all wrong.* If you're a good person and do the right things, people take notice. The converse is also true. While you may be able to fool some folks in the short term, the truth will always find its way to the top. The fact is, moral character matters. Period!

*Truth is not what it seems, but what it is.*

Margaret Thatcher, the former British prime minister, said, "Power is like being a lady...if you have to tell people you are, you aren't." The same holds true for being an exceptional individual. While the 10 steps are still valid, here are 7 guideposts to reach those goals while maintaining your personal character. These will truly make you more marketable.

**Establish high expectations.** Set your bar high and don't lower your standards for anyone.

**Hold yourself accountable.** If you look in the mirror and don't like what you see, don't blame the mirror.

**Learn K through life.** Keep learning – even when you're busy. Everything you learn is like money in the bank.

**Build trusting relationships.** You gain trust by proving that you're worthy of it. People will test you in small ways before trusting you outright.

**Add value.** Focus your efforts on adding value rather than on promoting your achievements.

**Live with honor.** Refuse to compromise your honor at any price. Knowing what's right isn't as important as doing what's right.

**Be true to yourself.** Listen to your conscience. That's why you have one.

## HOW DOES YOUR PERSONAL BRAND COMPARE?

A first-rate reputation doesn't happen by chance. It's a reflection of who you are and how you choose to live your life. Personal branding is less a marketing exercise than it is becoming the best person you can be. That means investing in yourself, developing win-win relationships, living a life of honor and integrity, and adding maximum value to the organization that hires you.

The motto of the movie *Field of Dreams* said it well: "Build it and they will come." The same holds true for you. Build an exceptional personal brand, not through marketing but through moral character and personal achievement, and the world will beat a path to your door. :)

"

# FORGET YOUR *TO-DO* LIST AND CREATE A *TO-BE* LIST.

"

# TO BE OR NOT TO BE

When you get older and reflect on your life, will you value the things that you checked off your to-do list or will you take pride in knowing that you enjoyed a life well lived? In other words, shouldn't *who you want to be* take precedence over *what you want to pursue*? What could be more important?

*Do you want to* do *more or* be *more?*

## FORGET YOUR TO-DO LIST AND CREATE A TO-BE LIST

By determining *who you want to be* rather than *what you want to accomplish*, you'll be able to identify your possibilities, weigh your options, define your aspirations, establish your goals, and measure daily progress against your desires. Moreover, it'll help you know if you're proceeding on track or veering off course. Here are 11 aspirations worthy of your consideration.

Do you want to be a:

- Loving spouse
- Dedicated parent
- Trusted friend

- Proud citizen
- Valuable worker
- Selfless leader
- Positive role model
- Thoughtful neighbor
- Caring family member
- Faithful follower of the Almighty
- Happy and fulfilled individual

You may be thinking, "I want to be all these things." But what happens when you have to choose between them? For example, you may be forced to choose between going home to your family or staying late at work – yet again; defending your principles or following the crowd; doing something for yourself or for your kids; calling out a colleague or looking the other way. The upshot is that your actions say volumes about your priorities, as well as about yourself.

## WHO DO YOU WANT TO BE?

While it may not be hard to define who you want to be, that doesn't guarantee that your wishes will come true. While being a dedicated parent, a trusted friend, and a thoughtful neighbor are all admirable goals, they're unlikely to occur by magic. Good intentions are not enough. You have to *consciously* make them happen.

*When you do nothing, nothing happens.*

In addition, we get so caught up in daily activities that it's easy to lose sight of the big picture. That happens because day-to-day deadlines loom large, whereas nobody's pressuring you to step back and put things in perspective.

What does it mean to be a trusted friend, to raise good kids, to be a thoughtful neighbor or an exemplary role model? If you don't take the time to define the personal qualities and actions required to achieve these ends, it's likely you never will. How can you achieve your aspirations?

## BE THE AUTHOR OF YOUR LIFE STORY

As you contemplate who you want to be in life, consider the following:

**Make yourself proud.** Be a person of strong moral character, set high standards, and remain true to your values.

**Earn the respect of others.** Live with integrity, let your actions speak louder than words, and refuse to compromise your honor for any price.

**Live every day to the max.** Reach for the stars, but never lose sight of the garden that you grew in.

**Surround yourself with top-notch people.** Choose your friends wisely and be aware of the impact they have on your behavior.

**Make everyone feel special.** Bring out the best in people, treat them with dignity and respect, and make a difference in their lives.

**Build bonds of trust.** Be humble and kind, act fairly and be dependable, promote openness and honesty, and always do right by others.

**Construct valuable relationships.** Put others first, make your relationships mutually beneficial, and never win at the expense of a relationship.

**Lead by example.** Be an exemplary role model, do what's right, and always let your conscience be your guide.

**Live with purpose.** Believe in a cause greater than yourself. As the saying goes, "The real measure of your wealth is how much you'd be worth if you lost all your money."

When you find yourself, you'll gain a new perspective about who you are, what you stand for, and where you're heading. At the end of the day, your option is simple: Define yourself by accident or define yourself by choice.

To be or not to be? Now you know the answer. :)

"

MONEY CAN BUY *THINGS*, BUT IT CAN'T BUY EVERYTHING.

"

# ARE YOU RICH OR DO YOU JUST HAVE MONEY?

If I asked you whether a particular person is wealthy, you'd probably estimate how much money they have and gauge the worldly possessions they own. That got me thinking. If prosperity is defined as good fortune, why do we confine our definition to money and possessions? What about the strength of our relationships, the memories that we share, and the peace of mind that we enjoy?

## DOES MONEY MAKE YOU RICH?

Everyone views money differently. Some folks buy what they need, while others buy what they want. Some people use money to *measure* their success, while others buy things to *prove* they're a success. Some people worship money like it's the most important thing in life, while others are grounded – and keep things in perspective. In any case, one thing's for certain…many people are actually poor because the only thing they have is money.

*Money is only one form of wealth.*

Here are 10 factors, other than money, that contribute to prosperity:

**Noble character.** Character is the fingerprint of your soul. It's not what you *have*, but who you *are* that counts.

**Meaningful purpose.** You may not have the control to lengthen your life, but you can do much to deepen it.

**Abundant memories.** Material possessions get old and wear out. Memories last forever.

**Deep relationships.** There is no substitute for a close relationship. Appreciate what you have, while you have it, or you'll learn what it meant to you after you lose it.

**Celebrated reputation.** Your reputation is like a shadow, following you wherever you go. Protect it like it's the most valuable asset you own – because it is.

**Continual peace of mind.** Some of life's greatest treasures are immeasurable.

**Strong self-esteem.** Make yourself proud. You have to live with yourself for the rest of your life.

**Outstanding health.** Some things are appreciated only after they're lost.

**Deep spirituality.** Open your eyes. It's so easy to lose sight of the things that you can't see.

**Clear conscience.** Follow your conscience. Sleep well.

## WHAT DO YOU SACRIFICE FOR MONEY?

I am NOT saying that money is unimportant, but it *is* important to keep things in perspective. If you define prosperity solely on the size of your bank balance or the possessions that you own, you may wake up one day and regret what you've sacrificed to obtain that prosperity.

There's nothing wrong with earning an extraordinary livelihood. The problem occurs when money becomes an obsession and you forgo *valuable* things to obtain it. Here are two reasons why that occurs:

**Enough is never enough.** For some folks, achievements deliver only *temporary* happiness. They're never really happy unless they're winning, and when the winning stops...well, you guessed it...like an addiction, they *need* (or should I say, *want*) more. These demands force them to work harder and harder to cross a finish line that keeps moving.

**Keeping up with the Joneses.** For other people, money is a competitive sport. Proving they're successful is so important to them that they're willing to go into debt to feed their addiction. As a result, they don't have the choice of whether to work harder – to satisfy their money addiction, they're forced to.

*If you appreciate what you have, you'll never want for more.*

## BEING OBSESSED WITH MONEY IS A HIGH PRICE TO PAY

Life is about tradeoffs. If you spend time and energy doing one thing, you forgo the chance to do something else (unless you can be in two places at the same time). So choose your priorities wisely. Some folks think they can beat the system – and have everything they want – by going faster or working longer hours. They're sadly mistaken.

*Happiness is a result of balance rather than intensity.*

Money should never become the cornerstone of your life nor should it define you as a person. If you pursue money at all costs, the price that you'll pay is real. The fact is, money can buy *things*, but it can't buy everything. You're rich when you learn that some of the best things in life are free. Are you rich or do you just have money? :)

"

GREED CAN BE
THE UNWILLINGNESS
TO GIVE OR
THE WILLINGNESS
TO TAKE.

"

# DO YOU SPEND MORE TIME GIVING OR TAKING?

**G***reed* is a term that describes ruthless people with naked ambition and people with an insatiable appetite for riches – those who give new meaning to the word *selfish*. Greed evokes images of the rich and famous playing with lavish toys such as luxurious yachts, expensive furs, and mansions that resemble palaces. But greed doesn't always apply to those who have money to burn. There are many people who are all too happy to take.

> *Greed can be the unwillingness to give*
> *OR the willingness to take.*

Greed doesn't discriminate between rich and poor. There are many ways that greed rears its ugly head every day:

**Life's a spectator sport.** "Bystanders" who don't pull their weight are greedy people. While others work at a frantic pace, selfish people work hard to avoid working at all. They spend their days moving piles of papers on their desk or watching everyone else go crazy. These folks wouldn't lift a finger if their life depended on it. When a job is complete, however, you can bet they'll be first in line to claim the rewards of the effort made (by someone else).

**Gaming the system.** For personal gain, greedy people look for clever ways or loopholes to outsmart rules and regulations designed to protect the system. Although their actions may be entirely legal, greedy people evade their responsibilities by off-loading the costs to others.

**It's all about me.** *A Christmas Carol* is an 1843 tale about Ebenezer Scrooge, a stingy and greedy businessman who has no place in his life for kindness, compassion, charity, or benevolence. In modern times, you'll find some business executives enjoying an obscene year-end bonus and lavish company benefits while telling employees that the company hasn't done well enough to support annual employee raises. Why? "Because I'm worth it." But catch them in a down year, and don't be surprised when they ask those same employees to "share the pain."

> *Some folks are so busy stuffing their face*
> *that they don't see their neighbor starving.*

**You've got my vote (as long as it doesn't affect me).** Greedy people have strong opinions about issues but expect others to shoulder the burdens. These hypocrites believe our country should go to war, as long as we send someone else's kid; the deficit should be reduced, as long as it doesn't affect *their* pet projects; taxes should be raised, as long as the increase doesn't affect *their* pocketbook.

**Something for nothing.** Greedy people are first in line to ask for more, but last in line to put in the hard work to earn the rewards. They feel they're entitled to the "good life" – even at someone else's expense – and they're not ashamed to take it.

**Takes all kinds.** Greedy people take things that don't belong to them, even at the expense of friends or colleagues. This can take the form of bluffing their way to an unwarranted promotion or accepting credit for someone else's idea.

**Robbing someone's confidence.** Some people bring out the best in others, while selfish people focus on themselves. Greedy people take great pleasure in tearing down others rather than in helping folks feel good about themselves.

**Borrowing from the future.** Greedy people care about their needs *today* and kick problems down the road. They put band-aids on problems rather than solving the root cause; they maximize profits today rather than investing in the future; they borrow to fund their buying addiction and stick others with the bill.

While ruthless people with an insatiable appetite for riches certainly have an ugly personality trait, being a taker is just as unattractive. Maybe it's time to value not only where life is taking you, but how you're getting there as well. Do you spend more time giving or taking? :)

"

*WHAT* IS RIGHT IS A LOT MORE IMPORTANT THAN *WHO* IS RIGHT.

"

# IT'S TIME FOR GROWN-UPS TO GROW UP

Kids do crazy things, but we expect more from grown-ups, don't we? Unfortunately, that's not always the case. Folks scream obscenities at ball games, bully people on social media, and treat others with total disrespect. If you think this behavior is rude, insensitive, and tasteless, you're right. But why is it so prevalent? The truth is, some people behave this way for personal gain; some folks don't know better; and others *know* they'll get away with it – because they have in the past. Some grown-ups never grow up.

While some indiscretions were once considered outlandish, we've become desensitized to these actions. It's troubling that this behavior could have been avoided, but too many of us didn't speak up. Instead, we closed our eyes to the poor behavior and waited for others to make the first move. The consequence is that wrongs committed by enough people become the norm over time. We have no one to blame except ourselves.

*As leaders, role models, and parents, we must utilize every opportunity to reinforce the values that we hold dear.*

## WHAT VALUES DO YOU CHERISH?

Are polite manners a thing of the past? Should people honor their word? Is it Pollyanna to expect people to do what's right? I think not! But if we don't promote good values, don't be surprised when bad ones become the norm. "How do we improve the situation?" you ask.

First, we must modify our criterion of excellence. It's not *what you have*, but *who you are* that counts. Moral character matters!

Second, we must set high standards of honor and decency for ourselves. If you don't raise the bar for *yourself*, how can you demand it of others? When you're a role model, every message you send is critical.

You send a message by:

- what you find acceptable and what you deem improper
- when you reprimand bad behavior and when you turn a blind eye
- when you care and when it's obvious you couldn't care less
- when you adhere to rules and when you break them
- when you stand firm to your principles and when you blow with the wind
- when you preach tolerance and when you harass people who disagree with you
- when you observe tradition and when you abandon it

- when you complain from the sidelines and when you get in the game to change things
- when you say "no" and when your actions clearly say "yes"
- when you follow your conscience and when you bow to peer pressure

Third, as grown-ups, we must accept accountability for our actions – no excuses, no finger-pointing, no second chances. The fact is, personal responsibility instills humility, boosts self-reliance, and emphasizes the importance of making good choices.

Fourth, it is paramount to have a single standard of justice. The same *rules* must be *fairly* and *equally applied* to everyone – no exceptions. We're not doing anyone a favor when some people are required to follow rules and others are given a pass. When we bend the rules and make "exceptions," norms shift and poor behavior can be viewed as acceptable.

*What is right is a lot more important than who is right.*

Lastly, don't blur the distinction between right and wrong. Compromising our principles, even one time, can be a terrible mistake. If we want to live in a moral and civil society, we must be willing to discipline people or organizations even when it's inconvenient or unpleasant to do so. Breaking the law is illegal. Period. If you experience behavior that you don't want your kids to mimic, send your message of disapproval loud and clear. Don't let your silence be misconstrued as approval. It's time for grown-ups to grow up and start behaving like adults. :)

"

AUTOGRAPH
YOUR WORK
WITH PRIDE.

"

# YOU CAN DO BETTER

Did you ever complete something and get sent back to the drawing board? You thought you were finished, but someone thought you could do better. Maybe they found an error, saw something missing, or thought you didn't do your best. In any case, it's frustrating. Right? The fact remains – in most cases, the final product turns out better than the original. So, even though it's hard to acknowledge, they did you a favor.

Why do other folks give you a pass? (They say you did a good job, even though they know better.) Some people want to be liked, and they're afraid you might snap at them. Others are tight-lipped out of convenience. They know your work is flawed, but it's easier to say, "Well done" than to be the bearer of bad news. And still others have lowered the bar for so long they can't recognize the difference between good and bad. Ouch!

People aren't doing you a favor by giving you a passing score if it's not deserved. Instead of working hard to raise your game, you'll be lulled into thinking you're making the grade. Moreover, if enough people shield you from reality, you'll be living a lie – and forced to face the consequences down the road.

## IT'S FOR YOUR OWN GOOD

It's not a weakness to have shortcomings. The true failing comes from having a lousy attitude – evading feedback, discarding suggestions out-of-hand, or thinking that you know it all because you let your ego get in the way. You should always want to *do* your best and to *be* your best. If other people are signaling that they want to help you, don't turn them away. Listen attentively and thoughtfully, consider implementing their suggestions, and then apply that lesson the next time you're faced with a similar situation. Moreover, when you do your best in one area, you're more likely to adopt that approach in other areas.

*Don't submit unfinished work as complete.*

In addition, you may be signaling that you don't want feedback. As far as you're concerned, you're finished and want to move on. If you don't know your shortcomings, you'll repeat mistakes over and over. Furthermore, you may start settling for less than your best. While you can't see mediocre work, I assure you others can. Next time you're passed over for a promotion or fail to get a raise, you'll know why.

*Feedback is a gift that keeps on giving.*

## AUTOGRAPH YOUR WORK WITH PRIDE

You may think that folks who send you back to the drawing board are critical or mean-spirited. What gives them the right to judge your work? The truth is, they have your best interest at heart. They're the ones with the courage, honesty, and compassion to tell you like it is. It would be a lot easier for them to relax their standards and give you a pass.

One day, you'll look back and thank all the folks who pushed you beyond your limits. Although you didn't see it at the time, they did you a huge favor. They took the time and made the effort to make the investment in you. They helped bring out the best in you and make you who you are today. So rather than mumble under your breath the next time someone says you can do better, send them a note of appreciation and thank them for caring. The truth is, they went out of their way for you. The least you can do is go out of your way for them. :)

> EXEMPLARY ROLE MODELS BELIEVE IN THE POWER OF GOOD — NOT WHAT'S GOOD FOR THEM BUT RATHER, WHAT'S GOOD FOR OTHERS.

# WHO'S YOUR ROLE MODEL?

Everybody has a hero. Who's yours? I'm not talking about Superman, who can leap tall buildings in a single bound, or even Mother Teresa, who is larger than life. I'm talking about folks, like you and me, that you look up to. What makes them so special? And how do these role models influence how you live your life?

Some people draw an artificial distinction between heroes and role models. They say we idolize heroes, while role models are "ordinary" folks who cross our path every day. The truth is, that distinction is irrelevant if both of them influence our behavior every day. When was the last time you thought about who your role models are, what makes them special, and how you can benefit most from them?

*People need role models. Are you up to the job?*

## WHAT MAKES YOUR ROLE MODEL SPECIAL?

Why is your role model so rare, and why do you look up to that individual? Is it their moral character, the way they treat others, their overall perspective, or something entirely different?

Consider the following:

- Do you know the individual personally or is this individual a public figure?
- Do you admire this individual for their outer beauty or inner soul?
- Do you look up to your role model because of what they have, what they did, or who they are?
- Do you admire this person for their achievements or for what they've done for others?
- Is your role model young or old, a man or a woman, from a background similar to yours or entirely different? (Does that even matter?)
- Does the individual maintain a high profile or remain out of the spotlight?
- Is the person admired by *many* or only by a *few*?
- Has this person impacted just *your* life or the lives of *many*?
- Can anyone replicate your role model's deed(s) or is a special talent or expertise required?
- Does this person possess a specific character trait or is their entire disposition special?

## WANTED: MORE HEROES

When some folks envision a hero, they think *idol* – someone larger than life, someone who broke a world record, put their life on the line for a comrade, or who is continually in the spotlight – watched by millions of folks every day. That may be true. But there are also people that folks look up to who are *not* famous and don't even view themselves as special.

But they are.

Heroes and role models don't have to be rich, powerful, or famous. They don't have to look the most attractive, wear the fanciest clothes, or drive the most expensive cars. They are as commonplace as a family member, business colleague, or even the person next door. But they represent someone very special in your life and in the lives of others.

It may be a teacher who changed a kid's life, a coach who helped her players achieve greatness, or even a stranger who went out of his way for a person he didn't know. You, yourself, may be a hero or role model to someone and not even be aware of it.

*People who look up to you watch every move that you make –
so don't let them down.*

I have my heroes and you probably do, too. They're always busy, but they always find time to make a difference. They don't think they're special, but they sure make you feel that way. They're quiet and unassuming, but they can light up a room when they enter it. They don't flaunt their success because their achievements speak for themselves.

*Exemplary role models believe in the power of good –
not what's good for them but rather, what's good for others.*

People don't "sign up" to be role models; others naturally gravitate toward them and look up to them. Role models continually cast an aura of goodness that's terribly hard to ignore. They don't do things to seek the limelight or win kudos. They aren't perfect. And they'll be the first to admit that to you. They do things quietly and are often the only ones who know the good they're doing. But that's enough for them because they don't want, or expect, fame and fortune. They take great pride in knowing they're making a difference – and they are! :)

"

IS YOUR CONSCIENCE
GIVING YOU THE
SILENT TREATMENT?

"

# A SIMPLE REMINDER THAT COULD CHANGE YOUR LIFE

When you were young, you were told to clean your room, do your homework, and eat what's on your plate. (Nag, nag, nag.) But as you got older, you stopped receiving reminders on how to behave properly because the onus now fell on you. That's called being an adult. How's that going? This lesson serves as a reminder of how much your mindset affects your life – and the lives of those around you.

*Is your conscience giving you the silent treatment?*

## 25 REASONS WHY YOU SHOULD TALK TO YOURSELF

Do your habits serve as a positive tailwind or a damaging headwind? How many of these precepts do you follow every day? If no one's around to tell you what matters, maybe it's time to talk to yourself.

**Value relationships.** Invest in relationships to avoid time repairing them.

**Up your game.** Don't wait for someone to complain to address your shortcomings.

**Keep your word.** When you make a promise, you're not giving your word in erasable pencil, you're inscribing your commitment in indelible ink.

**Be accountable.** Accept responsibility for your behavior. If you make a mistake, learn from it and move on.

**Be self-reliant.** Before asking of others, do for yourself. It's your life to live. Own it.

**Make relationships win-win.** Winning doesn't have to be at someone's expense. Instead, identify areas where everyone benefits. That's a win-win strategy.

**Do your best.** Take pride in what you do. You don't have to *be* the best, but you should always *try to do* your best.

**Get the job done.** Stop thinking of tasks as check-off items. Do things right the first time so you don't have to do them again.

**Be courteous.** A smile says it all. It takes no effort to say "Good morning," "Please," and "Thank you." Make it a habit.

**Give without being asked.** Step up to the plate *before* someone makes a request of you. Surprise them with your kindness.

**Build long-term relationships.** Invest in relationships. Prepare to concede short-term wins to secure long-term gains.

**Be even-handed.** Don't ask for more than you deserve. Greed can be the unwillingness to give OR the willingness to take.

**Don't keep score.** Give without expecting something in return.

**Take care of your employees.** Don't wait for someone to quit to recognize how valuable they are.

**Be tolerant.** Be open to other people's beliefs and values rather than just accepting of your own.

**Be a good neighbor.** Offer help to someone in need. Don't wait for them to ask.

**Show some humility.** Be humble. Your ego should never equal more than one-half of your accomplishments.

**Be a team player.** Be prepared to make personal sacrifices for the good of the team.

**Speak out.** Wrongs committed by enough people become the norm.

**Be a responsible parent.** If you don't pass your values on to your kids, someone else will.

**Be grateful.** Stop taking things for granted. Appreciate all the wonderful things in your life.

**Show some manners.** You're not alone on this planet. Hold the door open, give up your seat, cover your mouth when you cough, and put away your phone. Thank you!

**Wait your turn.** Don't jump to the front of the line.

**Keep the fire burning.** Never stop courting your spouse.

**Be a good role model.** Don't judge others' behavior; examine your own.

## TALK TO YOURSELF EVERY DAY

You shouldn't have to be told to be an honorable person, to hold yourself to a high standard, and to treat others with decency and respect. These deeds should come instinctively. But if you need a reminder to live your life this way, maybe it's time to talk to yourself. On the other hand, if you're waiting for someone to open your eyes, consider this a friendly reminder. :)

"

IMPOSSIBLE MEANS
YOU JUST DIDN'T
DO IT YET.

"

# IMPOSSIBLE IS ALWAYS POSSIBLE

There are so many things that once seemed impossible but are commonplace today. It took people with faith, hard work, and determination to make these things happen. They didn't listen to naysayers or give in to the grueling fight. They put their heads down, followed their dreams, and refused to accept "no" for an answer. They believed the impossible was possible — And now, the "impossible" is a reality!

How do you feel about the challenge that lies before you?
Will you do what it takes to win?

**Anything is possible when you believe!**

— FRANK SONNENBERG

# CHALLENGES

> IT CAN'T BE DONE *FOR* YOU; IT MUST BE DONE *BY* YOU.

# FREEDOM AND PERSONAL RESPONSIBILITY GO HAND IN HAND

One of the most memorable experiences in life is obtaining your driver's license. The anticipation leading up to the event is incredible, and the joy of receiving that license is even better. It's fantastic to be able to drive, but that pales in comparison to the freedom that a license affords you. The same rings true about graduation – leaving home and living on your own. There's no one to tell you what to do or second-guess your decisions – unless you ask, of course. You're in the driver's seat – but buckle up – freedom comes with a price tag.

Some of the best things in life have strings attached. In this case, freedom is a blessing, but it's also a curse. YOU are the captain of the ship – and hold all the cards. You set your course, make the difficult choices, and determine what you're willing to sacrifice to achieve your goals. Every time you achieve success, you can take great pride in knowing that you earned it. Conversely, every time you fail, you earned that as well. The key is that *you* own your life – the choices, as well as the consequences. As the Bible warns, whatever you sow, you shall reap.

*If you're not willing to make the commitment,
don't complain about the outcome.*

## FREEDOM MAKES EVERYTHING POSSIBLE

The American Dream may mean something different to each of us. At its best, it affords each American the freedom and opportunity to pursue happiness according to one's own aspirations. At its worst, the American Dream can be squandered on shallow goals that offer little substance or satisfaction. For these reasons, when choosing your version of the American Dream, be *realistic* about your choices and *bold* in your actions.

Some people define the American Dream as living "a better and richer life" – where everyone strives to live glamorously like characters in *The Great Gatsby*, and where materialism and excess flourish. For others, it means living a life of self-sacrifice, such as pursuing a career that helps others or that offers their children a better life than they had. Still others may equate the American Dream with being the first member of their family to go to college, create a small business, run a marathon, write a novel, conquer a disease, or overcome an addiction. The possibilities are endless.

Others might view the American Dream as being more about the journey than the destination. That might include being a good spouse and parent, fostering a supportive relationship with co-workers, or simply maintaining a healthy work-life balance. Fortunately, our country doesn't define the American Dream for us, nor does it limit the number of people who can achieve success – despite what some say.

Whatever your definition, realizing the American Dream isn't always easy. While, in principle, it offers each person an "equal opportunity" to succeed, it does not guarantee "equal outcomes" – not everyone ultimately succeeds in their quest. So don't expect to wake up one morning to learn that you've become an overnight success. It simply doesn't work that way. There's no easy road to success. It takes hard work, determination, and commitment.

*It can't be done* for *you; it must be done* by *you.*

The fact is, nothing worthwhile in life is easy to attain without effort. If we want the next generation to be successful, the best we can do is invest in people by providing a strong family structure and instilling solid values and the powerful work ethic needed to succeed, backed up by a first-rate education. The rest is up to them.

## LET FREEDOM RING

If you want to know the value of freedom, ask people who only dream of having it – people who don't possess the freedoms that our founders granted in the Declaration of Independence: Life, liberty, and the pursuit of happiness. And yet, even though many people gave their lives for the freedoms that we enjoy, others now take these freedoms for granted.

Freedom is a very special gift, but you have to be willing to defend and preserve it. As Ronald Reagan said, "Freedom is never more than one generation away from extinction. We didn't pass it to our children in the bloodstream. It must be fought for, protected, and handed on for them to do the same." Stand up for your freedoms before what you *have* becomes what you *had.* :)

"

IF YOU FAIL
TO ADDRESS
TOOTH DECAY,
IT WILL COME BACK
TO BITE YOU.

"

# THE GLUE THAT SUPPORTS A HEALTHY SOCIAL FABRIC

Our bridges, tunnels, and roadways are deteriorating and continue to be in serious decline. But what about other things that aren't as visible? For example, if you fail to address tooth decay, it will come back to bite you. The same holds true for the spirit and soul of our country. Problems don't get better with age.

We have a crisis of moral character, and our social fabric is being torn apart every day. Raising voices, pointing fingers, and talking past each other won't solve the problem. We must restore our foundation by getting back to basics, reinvesting in our people, and reaffirming the ideals that made our country great.

There is no excuse for the greatest nation in history to be leaving people behind. We must stop *talking* about our problems and start *doing* something about them.

> *If we don't make it a priority, it won't be a priority.*

## **REBUILDING OUR CRUMBLING FOUNDATION**

The best way to strengthen the underpinning of our society is by fortifying its foundation so that people can lead happy, productive, and purposeful lives. The glue that supports a healthy social fabric is composed of the ingredients listed below, with suggestions for how you can put this into practice in your own life.

**Family structure.** Children require a happy, healthy, and stable family structure. As a parent, it's your responsibility to raise kids who have strong morals and who will be productive members of society. That includes giving them your unconditional love, being an active part of their lives, shaping their character, inspiring good habits, promoting the importance of education, encouraging personal responsibility, and most of all, being a good role model.

**Personal responsibility.** You have the freedom to choose, but you're not free from the consequences of those choices. That's your responsibility. Determine who you want to be; set the direction you wish to take; and focus your efforts on your goals. Be the master of your destiny with a vested interest in your actions.

**Mental attitude.** One of the biggest obstacles to success lies within each of us. Some people blame scapegoats for their setbacks and difficulties. The truth is, if you look in the mirror and don't like what you see, don't blame the mirror. Ability determines if you *can*; attitude determines if you *will*.

**Education.** Learning is as much an attitude as it is an activity. If you think the world is going to stand still because you're not interested or motivated enough to make an investment in yourself, you're sadly mistaken. Unless you learn something new every day, you're becoming obsolete.

**Work ethic.** Hard work builds character, promotes dignity, gives you control over your life, and promotes happiness. The converse is also true. When people are rewarded *without making the effort*, it reduces confidence, promotes dependency, and robs individuals of their personal dignity.

**Moral compass.** Former Senator Alan Simpson said it well, "If you have integrity, nothing else matters. If you don't have integrity, nothing else matters." That doesn't happen by magic. If you want to raise kids with strong moral character, strengthen your organization's culture, or encourage citizens to be productive members of society, don't look to change *their* behavior, examine your own. Lead by example.

## THE WAY FORWARD: REBUILDING OUR SOCIAL FABRIC

The crux of the problem is that we've become entitled. It takes hard work to raise a family; it takes time to invest in your personal growth; and it takes courage to do the right thing. But instead of rising to the occasion, and accepting responsibility for our lives, we expect others to do everything for us. And yet, we still expect the rewards that come from leading a noble life.

When people have everything handed to them, *without earning it*, they're lulled into a false sense of security and complacency that weakens their ability to function in the real world. They lose control of their destiny and become dependent on the kindness of others.

*Helping people too much only makes them helpless.*

On the other hand, when people rise to the occasion and accept responsibility for all aspects of their life, they succeed based on their own merits. Every day that they make the effort, they build strength; every time that they overcome a challenge, they build determination; and every milestone that they cross builds confidence. The hard work and sacrifice make them better and stronger every day.

Compassion shouldn't be measured solely by the number of people we help, but by our ability to provide opportunity for others to reduce their dependency, enabling people to become self-sufficient and helping them to realize their dreams – all of which is a giant step toward rebuilding the healthy social fabric of our nation. It can't be done *for* us. It must be done *by* us. :)

> IF WE DISREGARD OUR VALUES, WE'LL OPEN OUR EYES ONE DAY AND WON'T BE ABLE TO RECOGNIZE 'OUR WORLD' ANYMORE.

# EVER HEAR THE EXCUSE "EVERYBODY DOES IT"?

Executive greed, dishonest politicians, and celebrities living out-of-control lifestyles… You'd think their behavior would infuriate us. Instead, we've become so accustomed to these ills that we're becoming complacent and even accepting. Is this the world that you want for your children? If not, where's the outrage?

The truth is, every time we turn our back to this cancer spreading through our society – we're condoning it. Every time we excuse cheating, dishonesty, corruption, violence, intolerance, adultery, greed, and lawlessness, we become part of the problem rather than part of the solution. As Edmund Burke, the statesman, said, "The only thing necessary for the triumph of evil is for good men to do nothing."

Everyone knows this is unacceptable behavior, but we continue to wait for someone else to make the first move. It reminds me of a horrific incident that took place in Queens, New York, in March 1964. One early morning, 38 respectable, law-abiding citizens watched a killer stalk and stab a woman in three separate attacks in Kew Gardens and didn't call the police. According to *The New York Times*:

> "As we have reconstructed the crime," he [police inspector] said, "the assailant had three chances to kill this woman during a 35-minute period. He returned twice to complete

the job. If we had been called when he first attacked, the woman might not be dead now."

…The police stressed how simple it would have been to have gotten in touch with them. "A phone call," said one of the detectives, "would have done it."

The brutal murder of Kitty Genovese and the disturbing lack of action by her neighbors became emblematic in what many perceive as an evolving culture of violence and apathy. Is that who we are? Have we become too complacent, apathetic, or lazy to stand up for what's right?

Whenever there's a new incident, we become outraged and then it's out of sight, out of mind. Our politicians talk a good game, but it seems that they'd rather score points against the opposition than address the problem. Meanwhile, the media outlets spin the news to fit their political persuasions and score some rating points, and the PR folks follow close behind, like ambulance chasers, trying to find creative ways to put lipstick on a pig. And all the while, we quietly sit by, idly waiting for the dust to settle and for the chorus "Enough is enough" to ring out. Instead…after things settle down…you hear people reason it away with "Everybody does it," and like magic, that excuse is supposed to make it better. The truth is, if we don't stand up and protect the values that we hold dear, we have no right to complain when they disappear forever. As Alexis de Tocqueville, the French diplomat and historian, said, "In a democracy, people get the government they deserve." The same is true of our cultural norms.

## IT'S TIME TO SPEAK UP OR SHUT UP

If you find yourself asking, what is our world coming to? – you're not alone. I long for a day when trust, honor, and integrity are once again valued; a day when a promise is as binding as a contract, when integrity is as important as the bottom line, and when we do what's right simply because it's the right thing to do. It'll be a simpler time when a handshake means something special and when a good reputation will be as valuable as gold.

*Times may have changed, but our values haven't.*

Times will change only when actions have consequences, and offenders are held to account. If we disregard our values, we'll open our eyes one day and won't be able to recognize "our world" anymore. Thirty-eight people in Queens could have saved a woman's life by simply making a telephone call. We too can make this a better world by rejecting this lame excuse and shunning those who act this way. As William James, the American philosopher, said, "Act as if what you do makes a difference. It does." :)

"

ONE PERSON
CAN MAKE ALL
THE DIFFERENCE.
AND THAT ONE
PERSON IS YOU!

"

# CHANGE BEGINS WITH YOU

The world is changing every day. If enough people create a ripple for change, we can create a better future.

One person can get things started; a second person can create some momentum; a third person may influence others to join in. And, before you know it, you've created a movement.

Your choice: Complain about all the things that are wrong or be the person who helps to make them right.

## **ONE PERSON** CAN MAKE ALL THE DIFFERENCE. AND THAT ONE PERSON IS **YOU!**

— FRANK SONNENBERG

# RESOURCES

"

FINDING THE
RIGHT ANSWER
BEGINS WITH THE
RIGHT QUESTION.

"

# 35 QUESTIONS TO INSPIRE SELF-REFLECTION

When was the last time you paused to reflect on your life? You're too busy for that, right? Wouldn't you like to know if you should continue full-speed ahead or if you're veering off course? Here are 35 questions to inspire self-reflection. They will help you identify your values, discover your driving forces, challenge your behavior, and determine whether you should recalibrate your direction.

*Finding the right answer begins with the right question.*

## A MOMENT OF SELF-REFLECTION

1. Do you give it your best or do just enough to squeak by?

2. Do you place more value on relationships or things?

3. Do you spend more time thinking ahead or reliving the past?

4. Do *you* define *good* or let others define it for you?

5. What *wouldn't* you do for money?

6. How is the public you different from the private you?

7. Do you make as much effort exercising your mind as your body?
8. Are you a good role model?
9. Would you choose to be friends with yourself?
10. What criteria do you use to determine happiness?
11. If you could change one thing about yourself, what would it be?
12. Is your reputation *overrated* or *underrated*?
13. What are your top priorities? (Do you treat them accordingly?)
14. What are the most valuable lessons that you've learned?
15. Would you compromise your integrity to get what you want?
16. Are you a giver or a taker?
17. Do you think for yourself or follow the pack?
18. If someone wrote your biography, what would it be called?
19. What mistakes have you made more than once?
20. Are you more likely to accept responsibility or to blame others for your disappointments?
21. Do you generally try to satisfy others or to please yourself?

22. Is it more important for you to be liked by others or by yourself?

23. Do you buy things because you *want* them or because you *need* them?

24. Do you chart your own course or go with the flow?

25. How do you know if you're being true to your values or veering off course?

26. Would you rather be *successful* or *happy*?

27. Do you appreciate what you have or do you take things for granted?

28. Who are your role models? What makes them special?

29. Are you proud of the way you live your life?

30. Are you living up to your full potential?

31. What's holding you back?

32. What do you wish others knew about you?

33. If you could live your life again, what would you do differently?

34. If you could accomplish one more thing, what would it be?

35. How do you want to be remembered?  :)

"

PEOPLE WILL TEST
YOU IN SMALL WAYS
BEFORE TRUSTING
YOU OUTRIGHT.

"

# WHY DO YOU TRUST SOME PEOPLE AND MISTRUST OTHERS?

Think about why you trust some people and mistrust others. What is it about their behavior that makes you feel that way? Here are 25 ways to determine if someone should be trusted. Do these thoughts cross your mind:

1. "I can always count on him. He'd never let me down."

2. "She's the same in public as she is in private."

3. "His promise is as good as a contract."

4. "She's always willing to help others and rarely asks for anything in return."

5. "He tells me the truth – even when it hurts."

6. "She'd never say anything behind my back that she wouldn't say directly to me."

7. "He treats everyone warmly – even if they can't do anything for him."

8. "He spends more time telling me what he's *done* than *promising* what he'll do."

9. "I can confide in her. She can really keep a secret."

10. "She doesn't spin the truth. She tells it like it is."

11. "He's always on time. I can set my watch by him."

12. "She's objective. She always presents both sides of an issue."

13. "He has strong convictions. He doesn't blow in the wind."

14. "She's respectful, even when she doesn't agree with me."

15. "He'd never ask me to do anything that he wouldn't do himself."

16. "When she makes a mistake, she admits it – and accepts responsibility."

17. "I always know where he stands. He's anything but a 'yes' person."

18. "She a big believer in win-win relationships."
19. "He's a team player, always willing to make sacrifices for the team."
20. "She's a good friend. I can count on her in good times and bad."
21. "He's very fair – open-minded, objective, and even-handed."
22. "She tries to do what's right rather than what's politically expedient."
23. "He's not an envious person. He's genuinely happy for my success."
24. "She's the real deal – what you see is what you get."
25. "I never fear that he's withholding information from me." :)

"

IF GOOD WAS EASY,
THERE WOULDN'T BE
A WORD FOR BAD.

"

# 15 COMMON HABITS OF MEDIOCRE PEOPLE

Mediocrity rears its ugly head when people have a poor attitude, a misguided philosophy, or bad habits. Know the warning signs in yourself and take appropriate action to counter them.

**Lack of accountability.** You always have a clever excuse or someone to blame so that you can dodge responsibility.

**Complacency.** You made it to the top and think you can rest on your laurels and live off your past accomplishments.

**Victim mentality.** You convince yourself that everyone's against you and that success is beyond your control – so you stop trying to affect the outcome.

**Lack of candid feedback.** You rarely receive, nor do you want, feedback, so it's hard for you to know where improvement is needed. As a result, you never learn from mistakes.

**Low expectations.** You set the bar so low for yourself that you're pleased with mediocre performance.

**Poor reward system.** You've stopped trying because there's no distinction in your organization between exceptional and poor performance.

**Bad influence.** You surround yourself with low achievers. Unfortunately, their behavior is contagious.

**Lack of competition.** You're the only game in town, so folks have no option but to do business with you.

**No conscience.** Politics takes precedence over doing what's right, and appearances become more important than outcomes.

**Get something for nothing.** You're rewarded based on tenure rather than merit, so there's no incentive to keep up with the times or to go the extra mile.

**Poor leadership.** You *easily* achieve results because the bar was set artificially low. The truth is, when you tolerate mediocrity, you get more of it.

**Lack of commitment.** You dip your toe in the water because you're afraid to go all in. The result is that a superficial effort leads to superficial results.

**Crave acceptance.** You lower your personal standards to win social acceptance and become a member of the in-crowd.

**Think you know everything.** You put learning on the back burner and become obsolete over time.

**Apathy.** You've been underperforming for so long you don't even recognize excellence anymore. :)

"

THE ONE WHO
MIGHT BE HOLDING
YOU BACK IS YOU.

"

# 13 MINDSETS THAT MIGHT BE HOLDING YOU BACK

There are plenty of things that you want in life. While you may think external events are most likely to block your success, the real culprit might be you. So many people thwart their dreams without even realizing they are doing so. Is your mindset holding you back?

**Lacking self-confidence.** Some people are afraid to step outside their comfort zone and try something new.

**Remaining a creature of habit.** Some folks avoid rocking the boat. *We've always done it this way* is their credo.

**Possessing a poor attitude.** Some people have all the talent to get ahead, but it's wasted because of their poor attitude – their failure to go above and beyond the minimum.

**Fearing failure.** Some folks are more comfortable doing things the same way rather than sticking their neck out and risking failure.

**Being afraid to get on the horse again.** Some people are afraid to go near the stove because they've been burned in the past.

**Allowing money to seduce you.** Some folks are so driven by money, they'd rather remain in a lousy situation than walk away from it.

**Preferring to take the easy route.** Some people prefer a familiar situation rather than complicating their life by trying something new.

**Operating on automatic pilot.** Some folks prefer to operate without thinking rather than contemplate a better way.

**Obeying rules blindly.** Some people would rather follow the rules than think out of the box – even if those rules no longer make sense.

**Needing to win acceptance.** Some folks want to please others so much that they defer to the preferences of others rather than satisfying their own needs.

**Electing to follow the crowd.** Some people need the comfort and security of a group rather than trusting their own judgment and thinking for themselves.

**Needing to avoid risk.** Some folks have a real aversion to taking a chance. They're like a deer in headlights in the face of oncoming traffic.

**Refusing to accept change.** Some people avoid new things at all costs. You can't teach that dog new tricks.

If you want good things in life, you have to believe in yourself, step out of your comfort zone, and pursue your dreams with passion. The one who might be holding you back is you. :)

> **WHO ARE YOU TRYING TO IMPRESS? BETTER YET, WHY?**

# DO YOU HAVE A BIG HEAD?
# YOU BE THE JUDGE

Do you have a big head? Could you be labeled an egotist, a show-off, a blowhard, a big talker, an arrogant snob, a know-it-all? If your ego can't fit through the door, it may be hurting you in ways you've never imagined. The following list provides 36 signs that indicate your ego might be out of control.

## 36 SIGNS YOUR EGO IS OUT OF CONTROL

Do you:

1. Blow your own horn?
2. Think you're better than everyone else?
3. Always want to be the center of attention?
4. Believe that rules don't apply to you?
5. Dominate conversations?
6. Make fun of people who are less fortunate?
7. Always have to be right?
8. Go straight to the front of the line?

9. Show off expensive merchandise?
10. Think you know all there is to know?
11. Look down your nose at others?
12. Steer every conversation your way?
13. Believe you can do no wrong?
14. Refuse to accept advice or be told what to do?
15. Try to set yourself above others?
16. Refuse to admit you may be part of the problem?
17. Talk about money, nonstop?
18. Refuse to let people into your clique?
19. Post selfies – all the time?
20. Refuse to apologize?
21. Require people to wait on you hand and foot?
22. Put others down?

23. Think no one else played a role in your success?
24. Believe your own PR?
25. Think you're too important to give others the time of day?
26. Dodge mistakes rather than learn from them?
27. Interrupt others?
28. Think you have all the answers?
29. Disregard what others think? (What do they know anyhow!)
30. Worry more about appearance than reality?
31. Treat every disagreement as a threat to your intelligence?
32. Force your viewpoint on others?
33. Think low-skilled work is beneath you?
34. Play one-upmanship every chance you get?
35. Feel like you always have something to prove?
36. Refuse to think this list applies to you? :)

"

THERE'S A VERY FINE LINE BETWEEN TRYING TO PLEASE OTHERS AND MAKING SURE THAT YOUR OWN NEEDS ARE BEING MET.

"

# ARE YOU TRYING TOO HARD TO PLEASE EVERYONE?

Do you spend more time trying to please others or yourself? There's a very fine line between trying to please others and making sure that your own needs are being met. Don't wait a lifetime to satisfy your needs or you may regret it one day.

## SEVEN SIGNS YOU'RE TRYING TO PLEASE OTHERS RATHER THAN YOURSELF

**Are expectations real or imagined?** Do people make you feel obligated to satisfy their expectations or are you putting pressure on yourself?

**How hard do you try to gain acceptance?** It takes a lot of energy to masquerade as someone else. In fact, it's exhausting. Real friends accept you for who you are, not for who they want you to be.

**Do you compromise your principles to please others?** Listen to your conscience. If you're not ready to do something, don't let others convince you that you are. Remember, you have to live with yourself for the rest of your life.

**Do friends and family expect payback for their support?** Real friends don't keep score. They give of themselves without expecting something in return.

**How much time do you spend trying to look good?** Great organizations reward people based on performance rather than politics. Every minute that you spend promoting yourself is valuable time you could use to be doing something worthwhile.

**Are you being asked to give more than you can?** If you give generously of yourself, don't let others make you feel guilty. To some people, enough is never enough. People can make you feel guilty *only* if you allow them to.

**Are your expectations of yourself unreasonable?** Some people are perfectionists; they always want to give more. The problem is that they're tough on themselves to a fault. Do what you can. You're only human. :)

"

NOTHING IS GOING
TO STOP YOU —
EXCEPT YOU.

"

# HOW TO FIGHT COMPLACENCY

You're at the top of your game. Nothing is going to stop you – except you. Here are 12 ways to fight complacency:

**Don't let your guard down.** Give yourself a kick in the butt. If you're not up to the job, find someone who is.

**Stay grounded.** Remember what made you successful and what you've learned along the way.

**Create stretch goals.** Set ambitious yet realistic goals. Challenge everyone to do better and to be better. The fact is, if you spend your life coasting, it'll all be downhill.

**Don't be a know-it-all.** Know what you know and what you don't know. It's strength, not weakness, to seek advice from others.

**Welcome fresh ideas.** Invite fresh new thinking that challenges your perspective. The truth is, surrounding yourself with "yes" people is like talking to yourself.

**Learn from the best.** Never stop growing. Identify best practices and make sure to implement them.

**Compete with yourself.** View success as a journey rather than as a destination. Focus on beating *your best* rather than your competition.

**Fight against routine.** Embrace change. If it ain't broke, break it.

**Look for areas of vulnerability.** Ask "what-if" questions to uncover blind spots. Be your own customer. Find the cracks in your system.

**Never underestimate the opposition.** Wake up. Any military strategist will tell you that underestimating the enemy is courting defeat.

**Maintain momentum.** Don't let up. As soon as you achieve one goal, set another. It's easier to maintain momentum than to rebuild it once it's lost.

**Look to the future (not the past).** Take time to smell the roses, but don't spend too much time basking in the glory of success. :)

"

PROGRESS IS ONE STEP CLOSER TO EXCELLENCE.

"

# HOW TO GIVE FEEDBACK

Feedback should be welcomed rather than feared. In fact, we should thank folks who make the effort to nurture us with their valuable input – even if it hurts at times. Of course, feedback is always better received when it's properly presented. Here are some tips on how to *give* feedback:

**Make your input count.** Give feedback that is *factual* – based on hard evidence – rather than emotional; is *even-handed* – examines both sides of an issue; is *balanced* – sees the positive and the negative; and is *open-minded* – free from personal bias.

**Make the feedback timely.** Offer input soon after an activity rather than weeks or months later.

**Give feedback in person.** It's important to give feedback face-to-face, or via "Skype" if necessary, rather than by email or text.

**Give feedback *prior* thought.** Know the key points that you want to make rather than shooting from the hip.

**Provide advance notification.** Don't blindside the recipient by catching them off guard. Furthermore, ease into the conversation rather than hitting them with a two-by-four.

**Respect the recipient's other priorities.** Catch the recipient during a peaceful time of day so that they're emotionally available.

**Refrain from multitasking.** Before providing feedback, secure the recipient's undivided attention – free from distractions.

**Build people up rather than tearing them down.** Compliment people in public; discuss their shortcomings in private. Avoid shaming or threatening the recipient at all costs.

**Focus on the actions.** Base your input on the recipient's actions rather than on demeaning the person.

**Be constructive.** Make your feedback *actionable* rather than general.

**Be honest and direct.** Tell it like it is. This will ensure that nothing is left to the imagination.

**Present the facts.** Feedback should always come from firsthand experience rather than something you heard via a third party.

**Encourage meaningful communication.** Make feedback a two-way *conversation* rather than a *lecture*.

**Confirm understanding.** Make sure you and the recipient are on the same page before ending the conversation.

**Establish an action plan.** Offer suggestions for improvement and expectations going forward.

**Follow up.** Establish a specific time to review actions taken and progress being made. :)

> A PROPER TABLE SETTING PROVIDES NO PLACE FOR A CELL PHONE.

# WHAT CAN BE MORE IMPORTANT THAN YOUR CELL PHONE?

Your cell phone can be your best friend or your worst enemy. Are you:

**On a date?** Who's more important?

**Walking on the beach?** Are you working or on vacation?

**Eating dinner?** Does that count as family time?

**Pushing the stroller?** Are you bonding with your baby?

**Watching your kids play ball?** Will you remember this moment forever?

**Attending a business meeting?** Did you get the message?

**Crossing the street?** Do you see what's coming your way?

**Watching a movie?** Why is everyone staring at you?

**Driving the car?** What's more important, the text or your life?

**THIS IS A WAKE-UP CALL. :)**

"

WATCH WHAT YOU BELIEVE BECAUSE YOUR BELIEFS HAVE A WAY OF BECOMING YOUR REALITY.

"

# YOU GET WHAT YOU EXPECT

People adjust their behavior based on the way they see the world. Here are 11 ways that you get what you expect:

If you believe **today's going to be awesome**, you're going to be happier and more productive than if you fear problems lurking around every corner.

If you believe **people are trustworthy**, you're going to manage relationships differently than if you think everyone's out to get you.

If you believe **you can overcome any challenge**, you're going to view obstacles differently than if you feel you're doomed from the start.

If you believe **you're going to be successful**, you're going to view your prospects differently than if you think, "People like me never stand a chance."

If you believe **relationships should be win-win**, you're going to build partnerships differently than if you think everyone's out to get the upper hand.

If you believe **good people finish first**, you're going to behave differently than if you think you have to be ruthless to win.

If you believe **feedback is critical to personal growth**, you're going to receive it differently than if you think feedback means you did something wrong.

If you believe **every successful person encounters failure**, you're going to view mistakes differently than if you think failing makes you a failure.

If you believe **hard work pays off**, you're going to view tough days differently than if you believe your company's trying to take advantage of you.

If you believe **people generally try their best**, you're going to manage people differently than if you think people are generally lazy.

If you believe **life has its ups and downs**, you're going to view bad days differently than if you think you're the only one with problems. :)

"

REMAIN TRUE TO YOUR VALUES. IF YOU DON'T STAND FOR SOMETHING, YOU'LL FALL FOR ANYTHING.

"

# MY BEST ADVICE

**Own your life!** If you look in the mirror and don't like what you see, don't blame the mirror.

**Make the investment.** There's only one investment that will never go down – an investment in yourself.

**Make good choices.** You have the freedom to choose, but you're not free from the consequences of those choices.

**Be careful what you wish for.** Success doesn't always guarantee happiness.

**Keep good company.** You determine the people you spend your time with. Choose wisely.

**Know the true meaning of success.** It's not what you *have*, but who you *are* that counts.

**Be realistic.** It takes many years to become an overnight success.

**Focus on the important stuff.** Checking items off a list doesn't determine progress; focusing on your priorities is what counts.

**Make the commitment.** You *don't* get what you want; you get what you deserve.

**Leave your comfort zone.** If you don't try, you forfeit the opportunity.

**Stop procrastinating.** Those who begin things, but never complete them, accomplish nothing.

**Set your mind to it.** Your mindset matters more than you think. *Ability* determines if you can; *attitude* determines if you will.

**Invest your resources wisely.** Saying "no" to one idea enables you to say "yes" to another.

**Remain positive.** "I can't" and "I don't want to" produce the same results.

**Take baby steps.** Incremental progress leads to long-lasting results. Focus on inches and you'll win by a mile.

**Set high standards.** If you're not proud, you're not done.

**Build win-win relationships.** Winning doesn't have to be at someone's expense.

**Keep your promises.** Every time you give your word, you're putting your honor on the line.

**Don't blame. Learn.** Excuses can be habit forming.

**Learn from experience.** Lessons in life will be repeated until they are learned.

**Show some grit.** Determination is habit forming; so is quitting.

**Start doing more by doing less.** Subtracting from your list of priorities is as important as adding to it.

**Learn to delegate.** Although the costs of not delegating may be invisible, the price that you pay is real.

**Stop whining.** Self-pity is like a disease…the condition worsens with neglect.

**You're only limited by your beliefs.** If you believe you can't, you won't.

**Plan for a rainy day.** Don't wait for a fire to locate the exit.

**Raise the bar.** When you tolerate mediocrity, you get more of it.

**Make *your* priorities a priority.** Don't try to please others so much that you lose sight of your own needs.

**Think before you act.** Don't do anything that you may regret one day.

**Love, trust, honor, respect.** It's so easy to lose sight of the things that you can't see.

**Be grateful.** Don't take things for granted. As the saying goes, "Appreciate what you have before it becomes what you had."

**Forgive yourself.** Mistakes don't make you a failure, but beating yourself up makes you feel like one.

**Be your own person.** Think for yourself rather than following the herd off a cliff.

**Check your ego at the door.** Those who serve arrogance as their main course will eat humble pie for dessert.

**Reject complacency.** It's easier to maintain momentum than to rebuild it once it's lost.

**Be practical.** You can't control the uncontrollable, but you can control the way you respond to those situations.

**Learn the meaning of *enough*.** Set your sights on what you *have* rather than what you *don't* have.

**Live within your means.** When you run out of money, stop buying.

**Be generous.** You don't have to be rich to give; your gift can be as simple as a smile.

**Let it go.** Forgiving doesn't mean forgetting, nor does it mean approving of, what someone did. It just means that you're letting go of the anger toward that person.

**Make every moment matter.** Moments, rather than possessions, are the true treasures of life. Material possessions get old and wear out. Memories last forever.

**Raise good kids.** Behind every good kid are parents who understand the importance of raising them that way.

**Live with honor.** Knowing what's right isn't as important as doing what's right.

**Lead by example.** You're a role model. Act like one.

**Remain true to your values.** If you don't stand for something, you'll fall for anything.

**Remain grounded.** Never lose sight of the garden you grew in.

**Be fair.** Judge ideas, not people.

**Live for a cause greater than yourself.** You may not have the control to lengthen your life, but you can do much to deepen it.

**Do good and be good.** Karma is like a boomerang. I hope you have many happy returns.

**Make a difference.** You may not be able to change the world, but you can change the world around you.

**Listen to your conscience.** You have to live with yourself for the rest of your life.  :)

> IF YOU CAN'T HEAR YOUR CONSCIENCE, TURN UP THE VOLUME.

# ABOUT THE AUTHOR

Frank Sonnenberg is an award-winning author and a well-known advocate for moral character, personal values, and personal responsibility. He has written 12 books and has been named one of "America's Top 100 Thought Leaders" and one of "America's Most Influential Small Business Experts." Frank has served on several boards and has consulted to some of the largest and most respected companies in the world.

Additionally, his blog — FrankSonnenbergOnline — has attracted millions of readers worldwide. It was recently recognized as one of the "Best Leadership Blogs," "Best Self-Improvement and Personal Development Blogs," and "Best Inspirational Blogs" in the world.

# OTHER TITLES FROM FRANK SONNENBERG

## VALUES TO LIVE BY
Know What Matters Most and Let It Be Your Guide

## BECOME
Unleash the Power of Moral Character and Be Proud of the Life You Choose

## LEADERSHIP BY EXAMPLE
Be a Role Model Who Inspires Greatness in Others

## THE PATH TO A MEANINGFUL LIFE

## SOUL FOOD
Change Your Thinking, Change Your Life

## BOOKSMART
Hundreds of Real-World Lessons for Success and Happiness

## FOLLOW YOUR CONSCIENCE
Make a Difference in Your Life & in the Lives of Others

## MANAGING WITH A CONSCIENCE (SECOND EDITION)
How to Improve Performance Through Integrity, Trust, and Commitment

## IT'S THE THOUGHT THAT COUNTS
Over 100 Thought-Provoking Lessons to Inspire a Richer Life

## MARKETING TO WIN
Strategies for Building Competitive Advantage in Service Industries

Printed in Great Britain
by Amazon